SHAUN S. YATES

OVER-EFFICIENCY IN THE LOWER CRIMINAL COURTS

Understanding a Key Problem and How to Fix It

BRISTOL
UNIVERSITY
PRESS

First published in Great Britain in 2024 by

Bristol University Press
University of Bristol
1–9 Old Park Hill
Bristol
BS2 8BB
UK
t: +44 (0)117 374 6645
e: bup-info@bristol.ac.uk

Details of international sales and distribution partners are available at bristoluniversitypress.co.uk

British Library Cataloguing in Publication Data
A catalogue record for this book is available from the British Library

ISBN 978-1-5292-3639-2 hardcover
ISBN 978-1-5292-3640-8 ePub
ISBN 978-1-5292-3641-5 ePdf

Cover design: Blu Inc
Front cover image: iStock/Paul Campbell
Bristol University Press uses environmentally responsible print partners.
Printed and bound in Great Britain by CPI Group (UK) Ltd, Croydon, CR0 4YY

FSC
www.fsc.org
MIX
Paper | Supporting responsible forestry
FSC® C013604

Contents

one	**Introduction**	**1**
	1.1 Introduction	1
	1.2 A revised theoretical framework	3
	1.3 Quality of justice, efficiency and over-efficiency	6
	1.4 The study	10
two	**The Modern History of Summary Justice Efficiency**	**12**
	2.1 Introduction	12
	2.2 Neoliberalism, New Public Management and post-managerialism	13
	2.3 New Labour, austerity and the Conservative government	16
	2.4 Significant court process reforms	20
	2.5 Summary	30
three	**Speed-Focused Managerialism**	**32**
	3.1 Introduction	32
	3.2 District judges and magistrates as managerial leaders	32
	3.3 Solicitors' cooperative case management	38
	3.4 The workgroup's management of defendants	45
	3.5 Summary	53
four	**Standardized Defendant Processes**	**55**
	4.1 Introduction	55
	4.2 Underused mental health diversion processes	56
	4.3 Under-specialized processes for substance-related offending	60
	4.4 Absent multiple disadvantage-addressing processes	70
	4.5 Summary	76
five	**Court Users' Procedural Adversity**	**79**
	5.1 Introduction	79

	5.2 Adversity from oral evidence procedures	79
	5.3 Adverse externalities for defendants	83
	5.4 Summary	88
six	**Overcoming Over-Efficiency**	**90**
	6.1 Introduction	90
	6.2 Slower justice is better justice (in the right places!)	91
	6.3 Less standardization, more specialization	99
	6.4 Efficiency as an adversity-free process	104
	6.5 Reforms recommendations	108
	6.6 Future research directions	112
	6.7 What does the future of the criminal courts look like?	118

Notes 120

References 125

Index 138

ONE

Introduction

1.1 Introduction

While efficiency is widely coveted by many modern institutions, this is especially true of the lower criminal courts of England and Wales (the magistrates' courts). This is largely because of the scale and subsequent impact of these courts on society. More than 95 per cent of all criminal cases begin and end in these courts, processing some 1.1 million cases every year (Sturge, 2023). This level of work helps explain the ~£548 million annual expenditure of His Majesty's Courts and Tribunals Service (HMCTS), which oversees the running of the lower criminal courts (National Audit Office, 2016). It is also worth recognizing that since 2016, HMCTS has received an additional £1.3 billion in reform funding (National Audit Office, 2023). In view of this large workload and financial cost, government reports have regularly emphasized the importance of efficiency in the magistrates' courts; indeed, they must operate efficiently to avoid an overwhelming backlog of unresolved cases and to ensure the financial health of the criminal justice system (discussed in Ministry of Justice, 2012; Leveson, 2015a; House of Commons Committee of Public Accounts, 2023). It is concerning, therefore, that criminal justice reports have criticized the lower criminal courts for being 'painfully slow' (Magistrates Association, 2022: 26), 'inconvenient' (Brodie, 2011: 11), and simply 'not good value for money' (Ministry of Justice, 2016a: 49). This need for greater efficiency has focused researchers' attention on investigating, designing and implementing a variety of pro-efficiency reforms. This is to the extent that, in recent decades, efficiency has become the defining issue of the lower criminal court literature.

Since the turn of the century, there have been numerous policy reform initiatives that have aimed to improve the efficiency of the summary justice process (the lower criminal court process). For example, in 2010, the sale of infrequently used courthouses and the reallocation of their work to centralized courts was projected to generate ~£15 million annually, with another ~£39 million in immediate savings (discussed in Cowie and Sturge, 2019). Meanwhile, the courts' integration and continued expansion of video conferencing (live link) technology since 2003 has aimed to increase the efficiency of the summary justice process by making courtroom appearances more convenient and proceedings speedier for all parties (including defendants, witnesses, victims and justice staff) (Ministry of Justice, 2016b; Crown Prosecution Service, 2020). As another example, consider the courts introduction and revision of the early guilty plea (EGP) scheme in 2010 which instructs judges to give a discounted sentence to offenders who plead guilty early in the criminal justice process (Ministry of Justice, 2012; Sentencing Council, 2017). The goal of the EGP scheme has been to motivate offenders to be forthright in their guilt, thereby allowing the courts to more speedily dispose of cases (see Ministry of Justice, 2012; Sentencing Council, 2016, 2017; also see Rossetti, 2015). Certainly, reforms such as these demonstrate how efficiency has been a key value that has shaped the contemporary summary justice process.

These large-scale changes bring into question what it means to be efficient when the lower criminal courts deliver justice. Is it efficient if the courts make cost-savings but, as a consequence, there are fewer local and accessible courthouses for the public? What if video conferencing technology allows the courts to achieve efficiency in speediness terms but, at the same time, court staff remotely mute defendants' microphones, preventing them from effectively participating in proceedings? Is it efficient if the courts dispose of a greater volume of cases if it also means that the courts increase the likelihood of imprisoning the innocent? Such questions prompt thinkers to scrutinize how efficiency-focused practices may be undesirable (or be for 'over-efficiency').

Over-efficiency is the key concept that the present book brings to readers. This case-study utilizes real-world observational data from a lower criminal courthouse to demonstrate how efficiency-focused practices can undermine the quality of justice. At the same time, this book offers tentative policy reform recommendations which aim to remedy such problematic over-efficiency practices. In doing so, this book aims to be valuable for policy reformers and students interested in the criminal justice system: that is, to sensitize such thinkers to the pitfalls of a justice process that is uncritically committed to efficiency.

1.2 A revised theoretical framework

This book makes a distinction between practices that are for efficiency and those practices that are for over-efficiency. While the prior is normatively desirable, the latter is not. To explain why this is the case, this chapter must first explain the seminal work of Packer (1968) and MacDonald's (2008) subsequent revisions, as these works establish the broad theoretical framework of the book. Indeed, the ideas of these thinkers are key for grounding the present work's conceptualization of over-efficiency.

This book builds from Packer (1968) and MacDonald's (2008) theoretical work, which frames the criminal justice process as representing competing social values. Indeed, in Packer's seminal 1968 work, he argues that:

> There are people who see the criminal process as essentially devoted to values of *efficiency* in the suppression of crime.

> There are others who see those values as subordinate to the *protection of the individual* in his confrontation with the state. (Packer, 1968: 4; emphasis added)

From the competing values of efficiency and civil protections, Packer (1968) constructs two models of the criminal justice process: the crime control model and the due process model. The crime control model is primarily for efficiency because it advocates for unfettered investigations by state authorities (such as the police) and the subsequent rapid disposal of criminal cases. However, this model also tolerates abuses of state power and the conviction of the innocent. Meanwhile, the due process model is primarily for civil protections because it is for rigorous checks on state actors (again, such as the police) and for ensuring that the courts uphold citizen rights. However, this model also tolerates slow, justice-delaying methodical processes. In this way, the two models of delivering criminal justice are in conflict and neither pure model is desirable in practice. These value-based models are useful for policy reformers because it allows them a simple heuristic, theoretical device to scrutinize potential changes to the criminal justice process. Rephrased, the models help policy reformer scrutinize the impact of changes they intend to make to the justice process, by prompting them to consider what other values must be deprioritized.

As MacDonald (2008) emphasizes, however, there are significant shortcomings in Packer's (1968) framework, which centres on how Packer conceptualized efficiency. Sometimes Packer (1968) frames efficiency as meaning effective police fact-finding; other times he uses it in reference to in-court speediness; and, in other instances, he frames efficiency as having a macro-level crime deterrent effect.[1] Indeed, Packer's (1968) conceptualization of efficiency is inconsistent throughout his work – it is unclear what he means by it.

This lack of conceptual clarity regarding what it means to be efficient in the criminal justice process has resulted in prolonged, circular arguments in the literature, where thinkers criticize each other for inadequately understanding what it means (or should mean) to be efficient. For example, see McBarnet's (1978) critique of Packer (1968), followed by Smith's (1997) critique of McBarnet (1981) and Duff (1998) (also see McBarnet, 1978; Ashworth, 1979; Rutherford, 1993). Indeed, in recent history, criminal justice thinkers have expended significant effort arguing that other thinkers have inadequately understood what efficiency means (similarly observed in MacDonald, 2008).

In an effort to clear the semantic confusion that exists around Packer's (1968) work, MacDonald (2008) has offered his own theoretical framework. MacDonald (2008) does this by arguing that social values (such as efficiency) are pluralistic, multidimensional concepts. To use MacDonald's phraseology: 'a simple yes/no approach to the different ways in which values are held, as Packer did, is inadequate'.[2] For MacDonald (2008), there is no single true or objectively correct account of what efficiency means. Rather, there are many different interpretations of efficiency in the criminal justice process. Indeed, MacDonald's (2008) multidimensional revision of Packer's framework is useful because it untangles some of the contentions held in the literature, where thinkers have (and continue to) debate what the 'real inefficiencies' are in the criminal justice process (see Marsh, 2016: 51; Nicklas-Carter, 2019; this is also discussed further in Section 2.4).

In providing greater clarity to his framework, MacDonald (2008) delineates between interpretations of social values (such as efficiency) that are either analytic or normative. MacDonald (2008) explains that analytic constructions of social values require the socio-legal researcher to utilize Weberian ideal-types (see Weber in Merton, 1952). Ideal-types are 'purely logical' theoretical constructs; they offer a 'one-sided accentuation of one or more points of view' (in MacDonald, 2008: 16).[3] Meanwhile, normative constructions of social values rely on individual interpretive judgments about what is desirable (or what ought to be). In applying MacDonald's (2008) theoretical framework, this book accepts that there are many overlapping and competing accounts of social values, including that of efficiency.[4] Certainly, a myopic, non-multidimensional approach to understanding the different ways the justice process can uphold social values is not useful: it unnecessarily restricts critical thought regarding what it means to be efficient in the lower criminal courts.

1.3 Quality of justice, efficiency and over-efficiency

For the present work, the concept of quality justice (or the substantiveness of justice) is normative and relies on thinkers to critically reflect on what values courtroom practices should uphold. In England and Wales, discussions of what substantiates justice is often grounded in values-based analyses of the Magna Carta (1215), the Human Rights Act (1998), the adversarial common law system, the Criminal Procedure Rules 2020, the Sentencing Council's Guidelines and the Crown Prosecution Service's Guidelines (see Auld, 2001; Barry, 2005; McConville and Marsh, 2015; Ward, 2016; Donoghue, 2017; also see Sentencing Council, 2017; Crown Prosecution Service, 2020). Within these various discussions, thinkers have argued that quality justice is paired to a number of values; these include: equality, impartiality, proportionality, open-justice, democratic representation, dignity, effective participation, accessibility, verdict-accuracy and accountability among others. As established in Section 1.2, such values can have multiple meanings (MacDonald, 2008). In this way, constructions of justice quality reflect how thinkers offer varying accounts of what it means to uphold equality, impartiality, proportionality or any other social value. To this end, quality justice is open to individual interpretation. While Raine (1993: 85) frames such open-endedness as a problem because 'the term "quality" is in danger of meaning all things to all people', the present work uses the aforementioned framework of MacDonald (2008; see

Section 1.2) to view such diversity as rational and theoretically coherent. Still, some further philosophical grounding is required, otherwise the present study's conceptualization of justice quality will be left unhelpfully ambiguous.

The present work accepts that practices which embody social justice values are for quality justice. This understanding has been similarly utilized by Ward (2016) and a range of other socio-legal thinkers (see van Swaaningen, 1999; Heffernan, 2000; Barry, 2005). Heffernan (2000: 51) succinctly elucidates what is meant by social justice in the context of criminal court decision-making:

> When we speak of criminal justice, we ask generally whether certain acts deserve to be punished and ask specifically whether a given act by a given defendant should be punished … [Meanwhile] when we speak of social justice, we ask whether the burdens and benefits of social life have been fairly distributed among members of a particular society. (Heffernan, 2000: 49, 51)

Therefore, when thinking about what substantiates criminal justice (what people deserve), this requires reflection on wider social issues such as equitable access to resources and opportunities (social justice). This relationship between social justice and criminal justice extends to courtroom outcomes (the criminal sanction) as well as the process (how court users experience hearings and trials). For example, criminal justice can be for social justice by providing in-court interpreters for non-native English speakers, or by providing legal aid representation for those who can otherwise not afford it (similarly described in Laster, 1990; Bhattacharjee, 2018). In these examples, it can be said that the process embodies the values of equitable participation and equitable representation. Thus, the broad concept of social justice aids the present work in its critical thinking regarding what practices are for quality justice.

The present work also accepts that values which support the concept of procedural due process are for justice quality. This is an approach that is similarly used by Ward (2016), who develops from the work of Heffernan (2000) while integrating some reflections on the Human Rights Act 1998 (also see Tyler, 2007; Galligan, 1996). As Ward (2016: 17) explains:

> I adopt the term 'procedural due process' and apply it in terms of defendants' rights within criminal court processes and procedure. In this way, interest is placed on how it applies to processes and procedures that are – or are not – granted to defendants in the lower criminal court system, such as the right to be tried in an impartial hearing in open court, the right for the accused to know the case against them, the right to legal assistance etc.

For Ward (2016), therefore, substantive justice refers to court processes that uphold the 'rights and procedures' of court users. Rephrased, Ward's (2016) concept of procedural due process frames the values of impartiality, open-justice, defendant comprehension and equality of arms as contributing to quality justice.[5] The present study likewise accepts that such values are for quality justice as they are applied to varying points in the criminal justice process and within varying contexts. And again, like with the concept of social justice, procedural due process does not offer an exhaustive list of values that are for justice quality. Rather, it provides a broad philosophy for thinking about how courtroom practices can embody varying values which result in a normatively substantiated justice process.

Among the broad range of values that connect with philosophies of social justice and procedural due process, efficiency also fits within the concept of justice quality. As established in Section 1.2, efficiency is a multidimensional concept; it can and does have many different meanings in the literature. The present work embraces varying constructions of efficiency, granted that they follow the broad philosophy that delayed justice is undesirable and that to 'do more with less' is desirable (Jones, 1993; David Cameron in Williams et al, 2014; Burnett, 2018; Judiciary of England and Wales, 2018: 13; also see Le Vay, 1989; Ministry of Justice, 2012). In this way, the value of efficiency tethers to procedures and outcomes which promote speediness, streamlining, convenience, waste mitigation and cost-savings.

However, the present work takes the view that courtroom practices that embody the value of efficiency (in its varying forms) are for quality justice only if such practices do not deprioritize values that are supportive of social justice and procedural due process. This is an important caveat that is missing in the works of Le Vay (1989), Ministry of Justice (2012) and the Judiciary of England and Wales (2018). To this end, the present work recognizes that within the concept of justice quality, the value of efficiency has a special status. Efficiency is indeed normatively desirable but it must play a secondary role to values associated with social justice and procedural due process.

In contrast to the normatively desirable concept of efficiency, overly-efficient practices are undesirable precisely because they undermine justice quality. Examples of such over-efficiency could include practices that deny defendants participation in proceedings in order to secure cost-savings, the omission of court users' rights to secure rapid case disposals or the use of artificial intelligence in place of human judges to streamline sentencing hearings. Indeed, in such cases the process would become 'hollowed out' or resemble a form of 'McJustice' where the 'best that can usually be said is that it is efficient and it is over quickly' (Ritzer, 1993: 36; Rhodes, 1996: 652; Bohm, 2006). To reiterate, the value of efficiency (in a variety of forms) cannot substantiate the justice process without first prioritizing values which are for social justice and procedural due process. In such unfortunate circumstances where efficiency is the priority value, the process becomes degraded: it is overly efficient.

A researcher's claim that a real-world courtroom practice is overly efficient must be grounded in empirical data. Indeed, to establish whether a courtroom practice is overly efficient or not first requires a researcher to observe courtroom proceedings and establish interpretively which values underpin a given practice and in what priority. From this initial value-based analysis, a critical appraisal can follow to argue whether such a practice is for over-efficiency. Accordingly, researchers' assessments of over-efficiency gain legitimacy by the rigorousness of their critical appraisals: their ability to logically evidence their assessments. To do otherwise can result in frivolous and tautological claims.

In conclusion, therefore, this book does not offer a definitive, prescriptive list of key values that are for quality justice. Instead, it tethers this concept to those varying values that are described in philosophies of social justice and procedural due process. Efficiency is a value that is also for quality justice; however, it must serve as a secondary priority when compared to social justice and procedural due process values. When a form of efficiency is prioritized above social justice and procedural due process related values, the quality of criminal justice declines – it becomes overly efficient. In establishing these three key concepts (quality of justice, efficiency and over-efficiency) and their relationships to each other, this work finalizes its framework for critically analysing courtroom practices.

1.4 The study

This work offers a case study of a single English magistrates' courthouse. It utilizes novel stenographic data that the researcher collected from 66 days of court observations over a 6-month period. From these observations, this work draws attention to practices within the summary justice process (the lower criminal courts process). The findings of this work are presented thematically across three chapters (Chapters 3, 4 and 5). In critically discussing these efficiency-related practices, this work offers policy reform recommendations to improve the criminal justice process.

While this study will be of interest to thinkers who are concerned with improving the quality of the criminal justice process, this work is particularly directed towards policy makers and researchers (and perhaps the ambitious student!). Consequently, the writing style of this work is succinct and forensic. Indeed, this work presents its findings by first systematically detailing each thematic observation from the courtroom (see Chapter 3, 4 and 5). Following this, the work separately and in an equally systematic way critically analyses these thematic observations (see Chapter 6). The result is that readers gain unambiguous, evidence-based insights into how the researcher justifies their policy reform recommendations. While critics may argue that this writing style is dry, this approach also ensures the greatest clarity of understanding in the mind of the reader: it demonstrates how the forthcoming policy reform recommendations have emerged from a thorough and rational scrutiny of evidence.

TWO

The Modern History of Summary Justice Efficiency

2.1 Introduction

Before advancing further it is necessary to situate the present work within the established literature, to firmly locate where this research advances discussions of efficiency in the summary justice process. To achieve this, Section 2.2 begins by offering an explanation of the rise of neoliberalism as an ideology in the UK. Within this discussion, the present work focuses on the rise of New Public Management (NPM), which has impacted English and Welsh public services. From here, this chapter explains the laudable but limited vision of Raine and Willson (1997) regarding 'post-managerialism', which argues for a departure from the economic and actuarially-focused managerialism of the 1990s. Developing further, Section 2.3 discusses how the changing political parties (notably New Labour and the Conservative governments) from the 1990s onward have pushed for greater efficiency in the lower criminal courts. Section 2.4 provides further detail by explaining a range of significant efficiency-focused reforms as well as some of the concerns held in the socio-legal literature. In doing so, this section explores academic and reformers' varying and often conflicting accounts of efficiency. By establishing this historical, socioeconomic and political context, this chapter enables the book to situate its own analysis of court practices and policy reforms in the subsequent chapters.

2.2 Neoliberalism, New Public Management and post-managerialism

Neoliberalism emerged in the 1980s, when England and Wales (as well as other Western nations) embraced a more laissez-faire, free-market-oriented approach to governing the public sector (Harvey, 2005; Bell, 2011: 140; Wacquant, 2012). In practical terms, the government oversaw the reallocation of work from the public sector to the private sector (Harvey, 2005; Wacquant, 2012). For example, see the involvement of the private sector regarding prisons in the 1990s (Ludlow, 2015) and the probation service in the 2010s (Deering and Feilzer, 2015). Additionally, neoliberalism promoted the idea of a small government with the citizenry taking more individual responsibility[1] for their own wellbeing. Within this broad ideological shift, the style of management within remaining public services also shifted, taking on more business-like characteristics. The socio-legal literature refers to this shift within public services as NPM (see Hood, 1991; Walsh, 1995; Hood and Scott, 1996).

NPM steers public services towards free-market inspired actuarial measures of success (cost-savings, target-setting, time-trimming, waste mitigation and production output). This is in contrast to services relying on a sense of rectitude or due process associated values (originally argued in Hood, 1991; also see Feeley and Simon, 1992; Raine, 2001). To use the phraseology of Spigelman (2001: 2) from his Australian court study:

> Perhaps the most definitive characteristic of the 'new public management' is the greater salience that is given to what has been called the three 'e's' – economy, efficiency and effectiveness – in competition with other values of government activity such as accessibility, openness, fairness, impartiality, legitimacy, participation, honesty and rationality.

There have been many branches of specialist socio-legal research that have examined such competing values in the criminal justice system, not to mention the aforementioned work of Packer (1968; see Section 1.2). For example, see Feeley and Simon's (1992: 452) research on actuarial justice and the 'new penology', O'Malley's (2010) research on risk management, and Harcourt's (2010: 74) research on 'neoliberal penality' (also see Fitzpatrick et al, 2000). Of particular interest to the present study is the specialist NPM-oriented work of Raine and Willson (1993, 1995, 1997) because they have specifically discussed ideas of efficiency in the context of the criminal justice process.

Raine and Willson (1997) argued that the governance function of the criminal courts rendered it unable to prioritize managerialist values (including efficiency) like other commercial services. Indeed, as Raine and Willson (1997: 92) argued, the moral elements of criminal justice (including that of judicial independence and democratic oversight) have 'never sat comfortably' with NPM reforms that have prioritized economic concerns. While commercial services could be consumer-focused and able to set short-term, trending targets, the criminal courts serve a regulatory function in society which is inherently long-term in its focus. To this end, managerialist logic betrays the primary function of the courts. Rephrased, Raine and Willson (1997) argued that the courts' mission to continually provide behavioural and moral governance regarding crime is incompatible with a managerialist ideology that frames the court as serving consumers (the public) of a paid-for service who have trending, short-term tastes.

Despite the insights of Raine and Willson (1997), thinkers continued to emphasize the need for managerial values (including that of cost-cutting, speediness, waste mitigation, and so on) in the criminal justice process. Central to this debate is that the courts operate within a capitalist system and, therefore, economic issues cannot be dismissed as irrelevant. This is an issue that Sanders (2002: 327) emphasized:

> This barely needs justification. However important it is that criminal justice be fair and democratic, it is equally

> important that other public services such as health care, education, and housing be underpinned by similar values. Fairness and democracy in criminal justice cannot be pursued unconditionally otherwise there would be insufficient resources to do the same for other public services. The idea that 'you can't put a price on justice' has never been true. We can, we do, and we should. The difficult question is what *priority* to give to efficiency. (emphasis added)

On one hand, Raine and Willson (1997) have argued that if policy makers prioritize the value of managerial efficiency, then the integrity of the justice process will diminish. Meanwhile, Sanders (2002) argued that managerial efficiency is a priority because it ensures that the criminal justice process does not undermine other important sectors of governance. To this end, a portion of the socio-legal literature has been at loggerheads regarding how the value 'efficiency' should be prioritized in the criminal justice process.

Raine and Willson's (1997: 80) work envisioned a new ideological framework, 'post-managerialism', which had the potential to resolve the concerns of both pro-efficiency advocates and efficiency critics. In the post-managerial model of criminal justice, the courts would simply be simultaneously for 'fairness and security as well as efficiency' (Raine and Willson, 1997: 93). The way that these values would be balanced, however, is somewhat unclear. Raine and Willson (1997: 92) gave weight to the idea that a post-managerial criminal justice process would be grounded in a 'new moral base', which is essentially Packer's (1968) conceptualization of due process. From here, Raine and Willson (1997) did not explain or advance Packer's (1968) work regarding how the criminal justice process can actualize efficiency alongside other due process values. This under-theorization was to the degree that within Raine and Willson's (1997) work, post-managerialism was contrasted with ideas of crime control which they seemed to forget was 'essentially devoted to values of efficiency' (Packer, 1968: 4). To this end, Raine and Willson's (1997) post-managerial vision was laudable but somewhat theoretically underworked.

The present work's theoretical approach advances Raine and Willson (1997) by offering a more analytically sound understanding regarding how the criminal justice process should uphold the value of efficiency alongside other quality justice values. To reiterate Section 1.3, crime control and economic forms of efficiency are not inherently undesirable nor result in low quality justice, as Raine and Willson (1997) suggest. Indeed, crime-suppression and economically-oriented interpretations of efficiency are desirable but reformers should not deprioritize other values associated with social justice and procedural due process in favour of efficiency. In this way, the present work offers Sanders (2002) a more direct, rigorous response to their economic efficiency concern. Namely, the value of efficiency is important but must be put into context: it can only substantiate the justice process when other quality-justice values are upheld. Rephrased, and to reiterate Section 1.3, managerialist interpretations of efficiency (such as speediness, cost-savings and waste mitigation) are important but they must be second to the more important values associated with philosophies of social justice and due process. To this end, the present work agrees with Sanders (2002: 327) that values such as fairness and democracy should not be 'pursued unconditionally' in an absolute, strong-ideal-type sense;[2] and yet, the present work adds that reformers should also not unconditionally pursue efficiency. The values associated with philosophies of social justice, procedural due process and efficiency all work towards quality justice ends when ordered appropriately.

2.3 New Labour, austerity and the Conservative government

The New Labour government established the political foundations for the contemporary government's drive for greater efficiency in the summary justice process. The early 2000s New Labour prime minister, Tony Blair, was notable for his crime-focused manifesto. Captured within this ideological vision was a speedy, modernized criminal justice system:

> [O]f all the public services we inherited in 1997, the most unfit for purpose was the criminal justice system ... The system itself is the problem. We are trying to fight 21st century crime – ASB, drug-dealing, binge-drinking, organised crime – with 19th century methods, as if we still lived in the time of Dickens. (Blair, *BBC*, 2004)

In an effort to modernize the court process, Tony Blair's premiership oversaw the implementation of the Criminal Justice Act 2003, their key piece of legislation in terms of transforming the criminal justice system. This Act recategorized a large number of criminal offences from the slower Crown Courts to the faster magistrates' courts. Combined with the drive to be tough on crime, the Criminal Justice Act 2003 also introduced 'hearsay' and 'bad character' evidence into the court process (Ward, 2016: 4). While these changes sped up the justice process (conviction rates), these changes also raised due process concerns regarding the integrity of evidence (see Sanders et al, 2010). By prioritizing speediness over due process, the New Labour government set the contemporary political foundations for transforming the criminal justice system (including the summary justice process) into something more efficient.

The efficiency changes that were introduced by New Labour were notable for their rhetoric, which was pro-social justice while simultaneously being pro-efficiency. This is a point echoed by Tony Blair when he stated that, 'it is the combination of economic efficiency and social justice that marks this government out from its predecessors', and that, 'the old choice that you had to choose between economic efficiency and social justice no longer apply. You can in fact have both' (in Dillow, 2007: 10). This vision to have both economic efficiency and social justice simultaneously, without undermining or deprioritizing either, somewhat reflects the post-managerial vision laid out by Raine and Willson (1997; previously discussed in Section 2.2). As discussed in the prior section, however, Raine and Willson's theorization about what this meant was underworked, and a similar issue was present in the New Labour government's reform vision. Indeed, as argued by Dillow (2007: 22), New Labour engaged in 'pretending that trade-offs can be avoided' and this therefore prevented adherents from:

> thinking deeply about fundamental values. After all, if we don't have to choose between liberty, equality or efficiency, we don't have to think about why these are valuable, or even about what they mean. (Dillow, 2007: 22; this is similarly discussed in Barry, 2005, and Cook, 2006)

This under-theorization was reflected in New Labour's real-world reforms. For example, see how the Criminal Justice Act 2003 produced speedier case disposals through the introduction of hearsay evidence but also worked against the value of verdict accuracy (discussed in Ward, 2016). To this end, while New Labour's vision was laudable, their policy reforms were not in step with this vision and, indeed, their reforms prioritized efficiency over that of quality justice values. Ultimately, they did not offer a coherent vision for what it would mean for the criminal justice process to uphold both efficiency and social justice values in a way that would promote quality justice.

The 2007/8 financial crash resulted in a fresh government push for efficiency-focused criminal justice policies, which especially targeted the summary justice process. Following the global financial crash of 2007/8, the government of England and Wales sought to secure financial stability through implementing 'cuts' to public services (Leveson, 2015b;

Nicklas-Carter, 2019: 9). As previously mentioned, the lower criminal courts process more than 95 per cent of all criminal cases and, as a result, these courts demand a large amount of resources (Sanders, 2002; Ashworth and Redmayne, 2010). In view of this, government budgeteers took the view that the lower criminal courts, the magistrates' courts of England and Wales, should be a point of focus when implementing efficiency-focused austerity measures (Nicklas-Carter, 2019). Efficiency, in this austerity context, simply meant cost-savings. Furthermore, as reported in the Ministry of Justice's (2013) *Transform the CJS* strategy action plan, efficiency was to be the primary value that the courts should uphold. Indeed, 'we cannot hope to achieve our shared outcomes unless we have a more efficient system' (Ministry of Justice, 2013: 14; also see Leveson, 2015b). Continuing from New Labour, therefore, the austerity-era government prioritized the value of managerial efficiency in the summary justice process above other quality-ensuring values.

During this period, the coalition government and subsequent Conservative governments continued to emphasize greater efficiency in the criminal courts. This drive for greater efficiency was captured under the slogan 'do more with less' and, perhaps more famously, in David Cameron's 2010 'Big Society' speech (in Williams et al, 2014: 2805; also see Judiciary of England and Wales, 2018: 13). Under the banner of the Big Society, the government emphasized that community and voluntary services should play a greater role in the criminal justice process (relieving pressures on the courts). This form of efficiency framed local organizations as being best oriented to address local issues (promoting justice outcomes) while also producing a financial benefit for government (cost-savings) (Williams et al, 2014; also see Morgan, 2012). In practice, these contemporary government reforms pushed for greater competition between legal firms for legal aid cases,[3] while simultaneously making the criteria for legal aid eligibility more specific (limiting some court users' access to legal aid support)

(Nicklas-Carter, 2019). Coupled with these changes to legal aid, the government pushed for solicitors/lawyers to embrace more pro bono work (voluntary service work) (Nicklas-Carter, 2019). By doing this, the government continued to prioritize efficiency, now in a wider range of criminal justice areas.

2.4 Significant court process reforms

This section unpacks some of the debates over the last few decades regarding the most significant efficiency-focused policy changes in the summary justice process. Of particular focus is how there are differing value concerns between criminal court reform thinkers. Where government-related reports[4] typically argue for greater efficiency, academic and non-government thinkers typically offer critical accounts of efficiency, arguing for reformers to prioritize other values in the criminal justice process. This section explores these contrasting accounts specifically in relation to: cooperative case management, the early guilty plea (EGP) scheme, live link technology, legal aid provisions, the amateurism/professional role of magistrates and, finally, the courts use of diversion and specialized processes. By means of this method, the section finalizes its exploration of the contextualizing literature that situates the present study.

Auld's (2001) *Review of the Criminal Courts of England and Wales* called for broad, sweeping reforms. It was Auld's (2001: 1) view that the criminal courts had a large capacity to become more 'streamlined' by more robustly promoting the value of cooperativeness between the prosecution and defence parties. Indeed, he envisioned that:

> There should be national standard timetables and lists of key actions for preparation for trial … the parties should endeavour to prepare for trial in accordance with the timetable and list of key actions appropriate to the case and to resolve between themselves any issues of law,

> procedure or evidence that may shape and/or affect the length of the trial and when it can start. (2001: 55–6)

This case management streamlining was set to tackle 'fishing expeditions' and 'warehouse disclosures' tactics used between solicitors (Department of Constitutional Affairs, 2006: 25; Auld, 2001). These tactics were undesirable because they focused less on achieving substantive case outcomes (an accurate verdict of guilt) and more on eroding the resources of an opponent. This led Auld (2001: 459) to affirm that 'the criminal trial is not a game under which a guilty defendant should be provided with a sporting chance'. The Criminal Procedure Rules 2005 (CPRs) codified Auld's pro-cooperativeness case management recommendations (Ministry of Justice, 2020; also see the Courts Act 2003 and the subsequent Criminal Procedure Rules 2020). Indeed, these rules made it binding for defence and prosecution solicitors to work together to ensure that the summary justice process does not encounter delays owing to issues such as unnecessary evidence/disclosure requests. Following Auld (2001), the Ministry of Justice (2005) provided further support for compelled cooperativeness between the prosecution and defence, arguing that it results in faster case disposals and, importantly, cost-savings (also see 'swift' and 'sure justice' in Ministry of Justice, 2012: 28, 45). To this end, Auld (2001) and the Ministry of Justice (2005) have argued in favour of greater cooperativeness on efficiency grounds (also see Leveson, 2015a).

In contrast to Auld (2001), Welsh's (2016) PhD work has argued that cooperative managerial pressures (which include the CPRs) have marginalized defendants in the court process, undermining the quality of summary justice. Welsh (2016; 2022) has argued that reforms such as the CPRs do indeed promote high-levels of cooperativeness between court staff and this, in turn, generates speedy case disposals. However, this cooperativeness produces 'routinization', where defendants are excluded from meaningfully participating in the process (Welsh, 2016: 104). Indeed:

> High degrees of co-operation tend to marginalise defendants from active participation in the proceedings … As work patterns are standardised in order to process cases as quickly as possible, the individual circumstances of defendants become less relevant … speedy case progression dehumanises defendants, whose cases are all managed subject to the same procedures even though they are likely to involve different issues and defendants are likely to have different priorities. (Welsh, 2016: 151, 172–3)

To this end, speed-focused, cooperative practices are reportedly deprioritizing values that uphold social justice and procedural due process values. Namely, court staff are less likely to engage with defendants' unique social circumstances (including their social disadvantage) because of such highly cooperative, speed-focused processes. Additionally, the process appears to deprioritize defendants' effective participation in favour of speediness (similarly discussed in ECEJ, 2016). Rephrased, the CPRs can erode quality of justice by favouring efficiency (speediness) over other quality justice values, resulting in the problem of over-efficiency.

Second, Leveson (2015a) has argued that the EGP scheme is for efficiency (speedy case disposals and resource savings) while also being for victim-focused justice (also see Ministry of Justice, 2012; Sentencing Council, 2016). Since 2003, the criminal justice process of England and Wales has emphasized that the courts should acknowledge and adjust an offender's sentence when they provide an early guilty plea (see Criminal Justice Act 2003, s.144). Yet, it was only in 2017 with the Sentencing Council's (2017) 'definitive guidelines' that the EGP scheme was formally established (also see Johnston and Smith, 2017). The EGP scheme provides structured guidelines for judges, instructing them to give a discounted sentence to an offender who pleads guilty early in the criminal justice process, in a tiered manner. Offenders can receive a third off their sentence (whether that be a financial imposition or custody time) granted they plead guilty at the earliest possible point in the criminal justice process. This scheme therefore averts unnecessary trials, which subsequently results in resource savings (Sentencing Council, 2017). EGPs also have the benefit of mitigating against the likelihood of a cracked trial – where a defendant pleads guilty just before trial. Cracked trials are for inefficiency because defence and prosecution solicitors expend resources preparing for a trial that does not take place (Sentencing Council, 2016; Ministry of Justice, 2012). Additionally, the EGP scheme works towards sparing witnesses and victims the emotional burden of attending court (Sentencing Council, 2016: 7; also see Rossetti, 2015). To this end, these thinkers have argued that the EGP scheme has contributed positively to the summary justice process by promoting speediness, resource savings and victim-focused justice.

In contrast to this position, some have argued that the EGP scheme erodes quality of justice because it promotes false confessions. Scholars like Johnston and Smith (2017) have emphasized that some defendants, driven by an overwhelmingly powerful fear of imprisonment, may resort to giving a false confession through the EGP scheme to avoid a custodial sentence (also see Horne, 2016). This argument reflects the work of Feeley (1992: 199) who has argued that the judicial process can be the 'primary punishment' for court users. Indeed, significant adversity can be caused by time spent in jail (remand), missed work or extra costs incurred from attending court proceedings (such as travel costs, childcare, reputational damage, and so on). In this way, a punishing process can motivate false confessions. Similarly, Adler (1987), while focusing on rape survivors, has demonstrated how the oral evidence-giving phase of the justice process has a capacity to re-victimize through practices that are emotionally demanding (also see Lees, 2002; Smith, 2013, 2018). Certainly, the emotional demands of the process should not be overlooked in terms of its capacity to punish court users as a whole (not just complainants/victims/survivors). For innocent defendants, specifically, this may compel them to give a false confession in order to avoid such a demanding process. American criminal justice scholars have identified a similar verdict inaccuracy issue in their court process when plea bargaining is involved, naming it the 'innocence problem' (see Covey, 2009: 73; Dervan, 2012). Despite significant differences between the American and the English and Welsh justice systems, there is a shared concern among scholars regarding the justice process's capacity to preserve verdict accuracy when plea bargaining is involved.

Marsh (2016) goes further as a critic of the EGP scheme, arguing that it promotes criminal justice inefficiency. Namely, Marsh (2016) argues that the courts' conviction of innocent individuals results in significant and avoidable costs to the public purse. To this end, Marsh (2016) frames verdict inaccuracy and wrongful incarcerations as a form of inefficiency. This criticism directly challenges Leveson's (2015a) vision of the EGP scheme, which claims that it champions cost-cutting and benefits the tax-payer. Consequently, Marsh motivates readers to be more critical in their thinking on this front, emphasizing that the EGP scheme is one of the 'real inefficiencies' of the criminal justice process (Marsh, 2016: 56).

Third, government thinkers have argued that video conferencing technology (live link) is simultaneously for cost and time savings as well as for court-user-focused justice (see Leveson, 2015a; House of Commons Justice Committee, 2019; also see Her Majesty's Courts and Tribunals Service, 2016). Leveson (2015a) has praised live link because of its capacity to secure hypothetical cost and time savings by omitting the need to physically transport prisoners to and from the courthouse. Indeed, Leveson's (2015a: 13) view of live link technologies were ambitious, as he argued that virtual courts should become the 'default position' for conducting most hearings. This argument of Leveson (2015a) fits into larger changes that governments have made in recent years regarding courthouse closures and courthouse-centralization. As Adisa

(2018: 6) succinctly explains, 'In the last 8 years, the Ministry of Justice have [sic] closed over 90 regional courts in the UK as part of its rationalization strategy to achieve economic efficiency'. Leveson (2015a) envisioned that live link could offset reduced physical, local justice with heightened electronic or virtual justice.[5] Additionally, Leveson (2015a) argued that the use of live link works not just for managerial efficiency but efficiency from a court-user perspective. Namely, it brings convenience to the court process. At present, court users sometimes make 'extensive and time-consuming journeys, for hearings that often only last a very short period of time', (Leveson, 2015a: 21). Therefore, by allowing court users to log in from a local computer (either at home or a detention site such as prison) they avoid the inconvenience of travel. In this way, Leveson (2015a) has argued that live link reforms are both for cost and time savings as well as for promoting the value of convenience for court users.

Conversely, other thinkers have argued that live link is unreliable and causes cost and speed inefficiencies (Donoghue, 2017; Gibbs, 2017; McKay, 2018). Gibbs (2017) has drawn attention to how live link's supporting technologies (such as that of internet connectivity, media players and speakers) frequently fail during proceedings. Consequently, cases involving live link are often relisted for a later date, resulting in inefficiency (case progression delays) (Donoghue, 2017; Gibbs, 2017). Additionally, Gibbs (2017) and McKay (2018) have noted that the justice system (court managers) have had to divert staff and resources from elsewhere to mitigate against such delay-causing failures, which may cause secondary inefficiencies elsewhere in the justice process. In this way, thinkers have argued that live link is not necessarily for efficiency, as it can promote delays and negatively impacts resource management.

Additionally, Gibbs (2017) and McKay (2018) have argued that the use of video-conferencing technology has obstructed court users' effective participation in court proceedings, undermining the quality of the summary justice process. Both

Gibbs (2017) and McKay (2018) have presented evidence of court staff intentionally muting court users' microphones during live link hearings, preventing live link court users from engaging with proceedings. Beyond these actions of staff, Gibbs (2017: 18) has argued that the use of live link has had a tendency to cause court users to 'zone out', that is, to become disengage from legal proceedings. Again, this raises questions regarding the usefulness of live link to support effective participation ends.[6] This reinforces the view that live link technology is not for quality of justice, as it does not support the value of effective participation.

Fourth, advocates within the government argue that the austerity-era Legal Aid, Sentencing and Punishment of Offenders Act 2012 (LASPO) reforms have improved the efficiency of the summary justice process. Specifically, Leveson (2015a) has argued that LASPO's changes have reduced the amount of paid legal aid working hours while maintaining service standards, allowing the criminal justice system to do more with less (see also Gallagher in Her Majesty's Courts and Tribunals Service, 2016). Leveson (2015a) suggests that this efficiency has been attainable due to concurrent efficiency reforms addressing waste and inefficiency. For instance, innovations like video conferencing technology (live link) have expanded the availability of legal aid solicitors, enabling them to manage more cases even with reduced paid working hours (Leveson, 2015a; also noted by the House of Commons Justice Committee, 2015). In this way, Leveson (2015a) has argued in favour of LASPO reforms as it promotes efficiency in the summary justice process.

In contrast to the government's position, some have argued that LASPO reforms have resulted in inefficiency. Doward and Dare (2016) have argued that LASPO reforms have made the legal aid application process more difficult for court users and, consequently, self-representation has increased (DIY defence) (also see Law Society, 2017). This is a problem because, as stated by the National Audit Office (2014: 14), self-representing court users 'lack the knowledge and skills required to conduct their case', resulting in typically lengthier and confused proceedings (also see Bowcott, 2014; Doward and Dare, 2016; Trade Union Council, 2016). Furthermore, DIY defence practices have caused secondary inefficiency costs in the criminal justice system (Trade Union Council, 2016). As Banerjee and Smith (2018) have explained, in the absence of paid legal representation, defendants sometimes rely on non-partisan legal advisers. This has had the effect of distracting legal advisers from their primary duties (also see Legal Aid Agency, 2018). As a consequence, some have argued that LASPO reforms have 'clogged up' (Marris in HC Deb, 1 January 2017: vol 619, col 119wh) the summary justice process, generating 'inefficient, slower and more costly trials' (Barendrecht et al, 2014: 86; see also Welsh, 2013, 2016).

Fifth, the government has implemented reforms to have magistrates 'do more with less', promoting greater efficiency in the summary justice process. (Williams et al, 2014: 2805; Burnett, 2018: 13). To encourage speedier case disposals, the Ministry of Justice (2012) has assigned new roles and responsibilities to magistrates. This has expanded the amount and types of work they can process. At the same time, criminal cases have increasingly been diverted from the costly Crown Courts to the comparatively inexpensive magistrates' courts (Ministry of Justice, 2012; also discussed in Ward, 2016). To generate further cost savings, the total number of lower criminal courthouses[7] and the number of magistrates have decreased. This has resulted in magistrates' workloads becoming, allegedly, more efficient: they must do more work in fewer locations and in fewer numbers (House of Commons Justice Committee, 2016).

Other thinkers have contended that these pro-efficiency changes have 'case hardened' the magistracy, undermining the fairness of the criminal justice process (Donoghue, 2014b: 940; similarly argued in Morgan and Russell, 2000; Sanders, 2001; Smith, 2004). Traditionally, thinkers have framed professional district judges, who have a wealth of legal knowledge and experience, as being case-hardened: for applying legal rules in an emotionally sterile or cynical manner to the detriment of upholding values of fairness and sensitivity for court users (see Boyle et al, 1980; Sanders, 2001). In contrast, thinkers have argued that amateur, 'fresh' magistrates are typically more emotionally considerate when handling cases and subsequently, magistrates deliver fairer sentences (in Donoghue, 2014b: 935; Morgan and Russell, 2000; Smith, 2004; Davies, 2005). To this end, critics have claimed that government efficiency changes have undermined the amateurism of magistrates, negatively impacting the quality of lower criminal court justice. Rephrased, thinkers have opposed the Ministry of Justice's drive to have magistrates do more with less, essentially, on over-efficiency grounds.

Ward (2016) contributes a layer of nuance to this debate by emphasizing that while modern magistrates serve in a lay legal professional style, this does not necessarily undermine the quality of justice they deliver. Rather, Ward (2016: 142) has emphasized the capacity of magistrates to act as 'social justice innovators'. Indeed, see Ward's (2016: 127) commentary regarding how one magistrate 'set up a supported hostel for young men coming out of prison with no secure accommodation to move to on release'. As Ward (2016) explains, this action of the magistrate emerged from their view that offending emanates from social disadvantage (a lack of access to housing in this case). For Ward (2016: 23), this summary justice practice demonstrates the 'embedding of social justice principles', promoting quality of justice. Ward (2016: 139) has further emphasized that magistrates may be more desirable than district judges because they bring the 'added value of shared decision-making in their tribunal benches of three'. To this end, lay legal professional magistrates may be preferable to that of professional district judges as they promote social justice and draw upon shared decision-making. This suggests that the current balancing of professionalism with amateurism is somewhat effective and is not, at least entirely, for over-efficiency.

Sixth, the socio-legal literature has debated to what degree the summary justice process should make use of efficiency-focused specialist courts, problem-solving courts and liaison and diversion (L&D) processes. Before advancing further into this issue, it is necessary to explain what these three concepts mean. As Donoghue (2014a: 32) clarifies, 'specialist courts' is an umbrella term:

> [S]pecialist courts are not necessarily 'problem-solving' in nature, as they may have a narrower remit, with objectives centred upon efficient and consistent dispute resolution ('fast track' courts), rather than addressing structural inequalities.

Indeed, while all problem-solving courts are specialist courts, not all specialist courts are problem-solving courts. A key difference between the two is that problem-solving courts seek to tackle structural inequalities as well as embrace therapeutic jurisprudence.[8] Problem-solving courts are not principally focused on speediness or actuarial measures of success, as specialist courts can be. Separate from both of these, L&D processes focus on redirecting defendants with severe mental health conditions out of the criminal justice system. These processes were nationally established following the Bradley report (Department of Health, 2009). As the Bradley report explains, the courts alongside other criminal justice authorities can and should play a key role in detecting and diverting such defendants out of the criminal court process to ensure just outcomes.[9]

The government's implementation of 'Transforming Summary Justice' (TSJ) specialized courts has sought to achieve greater streamlining/efficiency benefits (see Leveson, 2015a: 27; Crown Prosecution Service, 2015). TSJ courts are specialist in that they only process cases of a type, namely 'guilty anticipated plea' and 'not guilty anticipated plea' cases. In just processing these types of cases, the courts can produce streamlining benefits (discussed in Leveson, 2015a).

Leveson's (2015a) efforts to develop TSJ hearings has focused primarily on efficiency ends, not problem-solving (further supported with House of Commons Justice Committee, 2016). The establishment of TSJ courts is a direct outcome of the government's overarching focus on efficiency, which led to the discontinuation of broad, multi-agency problem-solving courts like the North Liverpool Community Justice Centre (NLCJC) due to their lack of cost-effectiveness (see Vara, 2014; House of Commons Justice Committee, 2016).[10] Moreover, these courts were purportedly ill-equipped to effectively handle cases involving dual diagnoses, such as those where mental health problems intertwine with substance misuse issues (Department of Health, 2009).[11]

In contrast to Leveson (2015a) and the Bradley Report (Department of Health, 2009), other thinkers have argued that government reforms should focus more on the development of problem-solving courts. In greater detail, Donoghue (2014a: 249) has argued that between the development of specialist efficiency-focused courts (such as TSJ courts) and L&D services, there is a service gap regarding 'short/medium term initiatives' that address defendants' social disadvantage (supported in Snedker, 2018a, 2018b). This is a view similarly supported by Bramley et al (2015) who have argued that defendants require a more ambitious, holistic approach that goes beyond current L&D services and especially that of efficiency-focused TSJ courts. Indeed, the criminal courts can act as a 'window of opportunity' for dealing with such social disadvantages issues that would not be properly addressed by either standard court process or L&D services (Donoghue, 2014a: 9).[12] Rephrased, these thinkers have argued that the summary justice process has the potential to more rigorously uphold social justice values.

2.5 Summary

In summary, the socio-legal literature demonstrates that summary justice reformers have continually pursued greater efficiency over the past few decades. More specifically, the courts have taken steps to secure greater cost-savings, reduce waste, improve timeliness, increase volume output/ case disposals, concentrate workloads and have relied more on volunteer work. In practical terms, the courts' drive for efficiency has manifested in the development of the CPRs, the EGP scheme, the courts integration of video conferencing technology (live link), legal aid provision changes (notably through LASPO), changes to the role of magistrates and legal aid solicitors and finally, the introduction of specialized court processes (such as that of the TSJ initiative). There have been four key government-related reports that have effectively spearheaded these pro-efficiency changes: (1) Lord Auld's (2001) *Review of the Criminal Courts of England and Wales*, (2) Lord Falconer's *Delivering Simple, Speedy, Summary Justice* (Department for Constitutional Affairs, 2006), (3) the Ministry of Justice's (2012) White Paper, *Swift and Sure Justice* and finally, (4) Lord Leveson's (2015a), *Review of Efficiency in Criminal Proceedings.* In contrast to these government-related reports, other thinkers (typically from the academy and non-government organizations) have raised concerns that such reforms are eroding the quality of the justice process, that is, they promote over-efficiency. The present work advances the literature by utilizing a refined framework (discussed in Sections 1.2 and 1.3) and novel court-observation data to argue in concrete terms what should be done about efficiency in the summary justice process. Indeed, in the following chapters, the present work discusses what practices take place in the lower criminal courts in real-world terms, what values are prioritized there, to what effect and, importantly, what reformers should do next.

THREE

Speed-Focused Managerialism

3.1 Introduction

From observing the lower criminal courts, the researcher identified three key themes (or overarching values) that characterized the lower criminal court process. This chapter presents the first theme, 'speed-focused managerialism'. It explains how staff prioritized the value of speediness during the in-court summary justice process through various micro-level, managerial practices. This chapter presents these speed-focused managerial practices in the following subthemes: district judges and magistrates as managerial leaders (see Section 3.2), solicitors' cooperative case management (see Section 3.3) and finally, the workgroups speed-oriented defendant management (see Section 3.4). These subthemes draw upon example extracts throughout to evidence the researcher's interpretation of the data. In doing so, this chapter demonstrates how the subthemes formed, and how these subthemes support the overarching theme, speed-focused managerialism. To this end, the present chapter offers insight into the daily workings of the summary justice process. Following this, Chapter 6 offers a critical analysis of this key theme (or overarching value), arguing that the observed speed-focused managerial practices rendered the summary justice process overly-efficient.

3.2 District judges and magistrates as managerial leaders

First, district judges were pro-active in leading case progression for speedy case disposal ends. This proactiveness is demonstrated in the following example extracts. In Extract 3.1, the district judge anticipates what the defence solicitor is to say before they finish their sentence and interjects, speeding up the case disposal process. Meanwhile, in Extract 3.2, the district judge anticipates the solicitor's concern and again, interjects as to speed up the court process.

Extract 3.1

District judge:	Why adjourned and not bailed?
Defence solicitor:	Yes … My client would like to seek
District judge:	[Interrupts] Technical bail?
Defence solicitor:	Yes.

Extract 3.2

Defence solicitor:	I don't know if you have had the opportunity to read the …
District judge:	[Interrupts] Yes, I am just reading it now. Can you please just allow me to.
Defence solicitor:	Yes sir, sorry sir.
	[A few moments pass. The district judge concludes reading]
District judge:	Yes, Mr Solicitor?
Defence solicitor:	So, sir, in relation to …

These examples demonstrate how district judges used a firm tone to control conversational turn-taking. The result was that district judges proactively omitted any unnecessary conversational exchanges between themselves and other members of the workgroup. In doing so, judges embodied a leadership character, that is, district judges rallied the court workgroup to deliver speedy justice.

Second, district judges' leadership embodied an intimidating character, which pressured staff to commit to speedy justice. Consider the following example extract where the district judge announces to the court workgroup to call on the next case. Here, the prosecution solicitor demonstrates non-verbal signs of anxiousness as they take a few moments to search for the required charge sheet to present to the court:

Extract 3.3

Prosecution solicitor:	[Speaking to district judge] I am just trying to open the document. Erm, I have a charge sheet but it's related to a charge in 2016 not 2018 … [Looks/scrolls through laptop]
	[Silence from all staff. A moment passes]
District judge:	[Inaudible/whispers to legal advisor]
	[I am close to the Crown Prosecution solicitor. I can see in her face, she is panicking/worried, eyebrows raised, hand around mouth. She keeps swallowing. Eyes darting across computer]

Anxious behaviour, such as that noted in Extract 3.3, was unique to situations where district judges were present. This workgroup anxiousness appeared to emanate from an expectation that they should complete case-progression tasks at a pace determined by the district judge. Indeed, as with Extracts 3.1 and 3.2, district judges were for speedy case disposals.

Third, district judges actively discouraged court staff from prioritizing any other value that was not for speed. Extract 3.4 exemplifies this. Here, a district judge scolds a solicitor for seeking to establish a duress defence for their client (which meant that the court workgroup could not dispose of the case that day):

Extract 3.4

District judge:	Okay. So, erect a skeletal argument, in 30 years of this business, I have seen one case succeed on duress!
Defence solicitor:	Erm, yes sir. [Sounds nervous/trembling]
District judge:	That's just my view, so erect a skeleton argument, show me on what basis you think you can succeed on duress.

In Extract 3.4, the solicitor prioritizes the value of adversarialism. This is evident in how they are advancing the interests of their client (the defendant) by seeking to defend them at trial. The solicitor's value prioritization works against speedy justice ends because trials are a lengthy process. The district judge in this example extract embraces a disapproving tone in commenting upon the solicitor's choice to defend their client at trial, suggesting that the district judge would have preferred a speedier plea of guilty at the current hearing. This further demonstrates the district judge's embodiment of speed-focused justice.

Fourth, district judges engaged in plea bargains mid-hearing to achieve speedy justice. Consider the exchange in Extract 3.5, where a district judge interrupts a solicitor mid-statement to encourage a defendant (the solicitor's client) to accept an impromptu plea bargain:

Extract 3.5

District judge:	Yes, sit down Mr Defendant. I have read the report … I will say today that he is doing well on a supervision and he is doing well. I have read the probation report.
Defence solicitor:	That is an advantage over me sir, I still haven't seen it.

District judge:	I am saying here now that he [the defendant] is doing well, as he has got a job and he is working well. If he accepts his plea then I will suspend the sentence, he is paying off his fines and I don't intend, to wish to waste the time of witnesses and victims. Would you like to have a word with him now?
Defence solicitor:	Erm, yes sir. [Leaves courtroom with defendant]
	[Time elapses. The defence solicitor re-enters court via main public entrance with defendant]
District judge:	Are we going to trial or not Mr Solicitor?
Defence solicitor:	No, sir.
	[The defendant enters the docket. The legal advisor reads out the charge and requests the defendant plea]
Defendant:	Guilty.
District judge:	Okay, good.

In Extract 3.5, the district judge encourages a defendant to plead guilty. This is evident in how the solicitor makes use of the time granted by the judge to leave the courtroom and speak to his client, rather than persisting with a not guilty plea. Again, this leadership practice of the district judge is beneficial from a speedy justice perspective, as a lengthy trial has been avoided.

Fifth, and in contrast to district judges, magistrates adopted a laissez-faire leadership style. Magistrates worked to establish speed-focused, cooperative spaces for solicitors and legal advisors. In greater detail, magistrates would listen to staff's workflow concerns, then, following this, the magistrates would retire from the courtroom space. This practice was for speedy justice as it enabled solicitors (both defence and prosecution) and legal advisors to work outside of the formal hearing process. In this less formal space, solicitors and legal advisors could cooperatively work together to find speedy solutions to case management issues. The following example demonstrates this laissez-faire leadership practice of magistrates and how they established cooperative, speed-focused workspaces for legal advisors and solicitors:

Extract 3.6

Defence solicitor:	Yes, your worships, this matter has made significant progress it may well be, in fact, that given a little more time, we could maybe be able to resolve the matter entirely, erm, by continue speaking to my friend. [Gestures to prosecution solicitor]
Magistrate:	Hmm. So, how much time would you need, do you think it's possible to resolve this matter completely?
Defence solicitor:	I would say, maybe.
Legal advisor:	Until 10 past 11?
Defence solicitor:	Yes, yes I think so.
Magistrate:	Okay we will retire then … *[Magistrates retire/leave the courtroom. Time elapses. Magistrates return to court from retirement/re-enter the courtroom]*
Magistrate:	Was that time helpful?
Prosecution solicitor:	To a large extent, I do think so, sir. The issue has now been narrowed down to a very small point.

As Extract 3.6 demonstrates, the magistrate facilitated for the defence and prosecution solicitors to convene privately instead of proceeding with the hearing as it was listed for the day. In doing so, the solicitors cooperated to 'narrow down' which part of the evidence they contested. The solicitors, along with the legal advisor, worked outside of the formal hearing process to resolve case management issues speedily. This allowed the formal (time-consuming) case management hearing process to be conducted in a swifter fashion, that is, the workgroup was able to largely omit a formal case management hearing. To this end, magistrates' laissez-faire leadership style embodied the value of speedy justice.

3.3 Solicitors' cooperative case management

First, solicitors would convene prior to a hearing/trial taking place to cooperatively resolve case management issues. Such practices embodied the value of speedy justice because solicitors' cooperative planning resulted in more focused (succinct) hearings/trials. It was normal practice for defence solicitors and Crown Prosecution Service solicitors to convene minutes (or even seconds) before a hearing began to discuss case management issues. The following extracts demonstrate this pre-hearing/trial cooperative planning practice of solicitors:

Extract 3.7

Prosecution solicitor:	Don't worry, I'm not going to try and do anything to try and ambush you.
Defence solicitor:	No, yeah yeah, yeah.
Prosecution solicitor:	... I don't think it's a lie, I just think that maybe she just misremembered it.
Defence solicitor:	And the thing is, I feel like Mr X is the most helpful to my client. So, I was like 'are you sure he's not here?' [Referring to the location where the crime took place] [Laughs]
Prosecution solicitor:	Yeah, it's; it would be an odd lie.
Defence solicitor:	Exactly. It doesn't help either side.

Extract 3.8

[Defence solicitor and prosecution solicitor continue watching the CCTV footage/evidence on a laptop. The two are shoulder to shoulder. They are both comparing written statements to the CCTV footage. The footage is also on a large screen overhead]

Prosecution solicitor: To me, that punch could be left or right. I can't really see that. [Gesturing to the computer]

Defence solicitor: So, what, what, what. Oh. He's pushing his hands off there.

Prosecution solicitor: Well, he is definitely backing off and then he clearly goes for him [pause] … I mean he's got [sigh], ahh he has resist [short for the charge 'resist a police constable in execution of duty'] erm. I'm not saying he definitely can but there is the argument that he can say he was resisting … I suspect that this is going to go upstairs [slang for Crown Court] on a 47 [short for a Section 47 assault charge], isn't it?

Defence solicitor: Yeah, I think so because this is arguably a category 1 because … [Words drop off/inaudible]

Prosecution solicitor: Yeah, yeah.

In Extract 3.7, the prosecution solicitor and the defence solicitor worked together to discuss the role of a witness's statements in the upcoming trial, concluding that the witness is unreliable for both parties. As a result, the solicitors agreed not to present this evidence and the summary justice process was sped up. Meanwhile, in

Extract 3.8, the prosecution and defence solicitors worked together to review the charge put to the defendant. In doing so, they discussed whether the case should remain in the magistrates' court or whether they should send it to the Crown Court. This practice similarly embodies the value of speedy justice because the solicitors worked together, outside of the highly procedural and time-consuming formal case management hearing process.

Second, solicitors would work together during pre-hearing cooperative planning periods to establish hearing/trial outcomes (including whether or not a defendant was guilty). These practices were for speedy justice because they omitted time-consuming, adversarial practices which rely on zealous advocates testing the strength of evidence. Consider the succinct example in Extract 3.9, which evidences how a defence solicitor clarified to the prosecution that they believed their client to be guilty, despite their client's plea of not guilty. For context, the individuals present in the courtroom during this pre-hearing planning period were the defence solicitor, prosecution solicitor and legal advisor, which is typical of pre-hearing planning sessions:

Extract 3.9

Prosecution solicitor:	So, is this a not guilty plea?
Defence solicitor:	For the moment. What a prat! [Referring to their client, the defendant]

In this example, the defence solicitor's announcement initiated a conversation regarding how they should plan the upcoming trial. This would mean that although solicitors pre-planned a hearing/trial, they would still take part in the formal, adversarial processes that followed. This rendered solicitors' adversarial practices pseudo in nature. Rephrased, following such pre-hearing planning sessions, solicitors would feign being zealous advocates for their client in the formal hearing process, as they had already indicated/established court proceeding outcomes with the opposing party's solicitor. In this way, solicitors' pseudo-adversarial practices embodied the value of speedy justice.

In further support of this analysis, the researcher observed two solicitors who explained that they were in favour of cooperativeness because it served speedy justice ends. During the observation period, there was a court user who sat in the gallery who asked two presiding solicitors, 'Do you two pretend to argue with each other?' (The court user seemingly made this comment because they arrived upon a similar interpretation to that noted earlier, regarding how solicitors performed in a feigned adversarial manner.) The prosecution and defence solicitors responded as follows in Extract 3.10. In this exchange, the tone was open and relaxed. This exchange occurred during the pre-hearing/trial period, while magistrates were in retirement:

Extract 3.10

Prosecution solicitor:	There is no point in not getting along with each other because otherwise it just makes it harder for you to compromise.
Defence solicitor:	Yeah, that's it.
Court user:	I think it's good, to rather make friends, rather than actually hate each other. [Laughs]
Prosecution solicitor:	Yeah, that's it.
Defence solicitor:	If you are going to have petty arguments then you are not going to be able to achieve much.

As supported by this example extract, solicitors performed in a feigned adversarial or pseudo-adversarial fashion. They favoured cooperativeness as this would cause speedy case disposal outcomes. Or, to use the defence solicitor's phraseology, 'If you are going to have petty arguments then you are not going to be able to achieve much'. Again, therefore, solicitors' shared prioritization of speedy justice drove their cooperativeness.

Third, prosecution solicitors' cooperative drive for speediness resulted in them rarely contesting defendants' mitigating factors. Consider the following example (Extract 3.11) taken from a domestic violence case which demonstrates the typical non-adversarialism of prosecution solicitors:

Extract 3.11

Defence solicitor:	He has elderly parents who are extremely ill … both mother and father have serious heart problems … he is effectively looking after his parents … due to conditions imposed upon him, he is unable to make contact with his mother as she lives very close to the complainant … still he has organized for another relative to look after his mother … sir, he is hoping to return back to his parents to help them, they are at the forefront of his mind, he has expressed his remorse, sir … he tells me since January he has not taken a drop of alcohol … so also, more pivotal, I will be asking you to consider that at the forefront of his mind is rehabilitation. *[Hearing continues until the magistrate announces the defendant's sentence. Prosecution does not contest the mitigating factors of the defence. The magistrate then formally concludes the sentencing hearing]*
Court user:	[Cries loudly] Everything she said about him is wrong! He doesn't even look after his mum and dad!

Legal advisor:	Well, hang on just, there [legal advisor is tripping over their words]. He [the defendant] may still be outside. Ms Defence Solicitor was just doing her job.
Defence solicitor:	I'm sorry, I'm just doing my job.
Court user:	He was laughing as he was leaving! Did you see him? He's got away with it!

In Extract 3.11, the defence solicitor presented a series of mitigating factors in a somewhat scatter-gun manner to encourage the magistrates to give a lesser sentence. The prosecution gave no contest and, following this, the magistrate delivered their sentence. By omitting adversarial contests regarding the defendant's mitigating factors, solicitors disposed of cases quickly. Following this, the court user was concerned with the accuracy of the magistrates' sentence, given that, to their knowledge, the defendant 'doesn't even look after his mum and dad'. To this end, the prosecution solicitors' non-contesting of mitigating factors produced speedy justice but it also resulted in sentence proportionality concerns.

Finally, and as a caveat to the previous points made in this section, the researcher gathered evidence to demonstrate that solicitors departed from cooperative, speed-focused justice when conducting cross-examinations at trial. This observation is noteworthy because, in the researcher's view, it demonstrates the limit of solicitors' cooperative focus on speedy case disposals. Solicitors of both sides would frequently make handwritten notes during their opponent's cross-examinations, seemingly preparing counter points or new lines of questioning. In the researcher's view, such committed adversarialism was also evident in how solicitors of both sides would eagerly interrupt their opponent during cross-examination. Such interruptions would typically happen when a solicitor believed that their opponent's questioning was irrelevant or unfair to their client. Consider the following extracts involving a sexual assault matter (in Extract 3.12) and a domestic violence matter (in Extract 3.13) which demonstrates solicitors' commitment to adversarialism:

Extract 3.12

Defence solicitor:	Screaming and shouting you were, weren't you?
Witness:	No.
Defence solicitor:	Just like you were in your 999 call, weren't you?
Witness:	No.
Defence solicitor:	You put your own son in the middle of an argument, telling him not to undo his seatbelt.
Prosecution solicitor:	[Interrupts] Is that a question or?
Defence solicitor:	It's coming now sir! [This exclamation is directed at the prosecution solicitor. A brief pause, then the defence solicitor draws their attention back to the witness]. What do you do after Mr Defendant tells your son not to undo his seat belt?

Extract 3.13

Defence solicitor:	[Directing cross-examination questions to the witness who is in the witness box] Well, in your evidence, you said that 'you didn't go out' but now you are saying that you did go out, and now you are saying that you changed your evidence.
Prosecution solicitor:	Well, I would appreciate it if my learned friend ... [Interrupted by the defence solicitor] *[The defence and prosecution solicitor talk over each other, building up to shouting over each other]*

As this demonstrates, solicitors were not absolutely concerned with speed-focused and cooperative practices. Instead, solicitors interrupted each other and drew their opponent's attention to the rules of proper procedure. To this end, during cross-examinations, solicitors prioritized the value of substantiated or true (rather than pseudo) adversarialism. As a last point of emphasis, the researcher only observed solicitors embodying true adversarialism during serious cases such as that of sexual or domestic violence (like in the previous example extracts). Solicitors did not demonstrate true adversarialism during less serious matters, such as that of littering or driving penalties. In this way, solicitors' sense of case seriousness determined whether they should prioritize true adversarialism over speediness. Indeed, in the researcher's interpretation, this was the limit of solicitors' prioritization of speedy justice.

3.4 The workgroup's management of defendants

First, the court workgroup strictly controlled defendants' verbal participation in order to dispose of cases speedily. When defendants attempted to speak freely during their hearing/trial, a member of the court workgroup would almost always interject. These interjections occurred because the court workgroup were primarily concerned with completing their work rather than engaging with the defendant's concerns. This frustrated defendants. Consider the following example extracts which demonstrates this frustration:

Extract 3.14

Defendant:	Well, I am guilty but …
District judge:	[Interrupts] Please sit-down Mr Defendant, I'm sure Ms Solicitor can explain for us. [Shouts] I said sit down Mr Defendant, this is what Ms Solicitor is here for!
Defendant:	Arhhh! [Sits down]

Extract 3.15

Defendant:	[Inaudible]
Magistrate:	[Interrupts and speaks over defendant loudly] We will order a collection order so that bailiffs will be ordered, if you do not make payment.
Defendant:	That's not fair.
Magistrate:	[Interrupts, shouting louder than before] It is fair!

Extract 3.16

Defendant:	[Interrupts] Can I say something please?
Defence solicitor:	No.
District judge:	If you interrupt again, I will send you to the cells. This is not a public forum shouting match. Am I clear?
Defendant:	[Pauses] I just wanted …
District judge:	[Interrupts] Am I clear?
Defendant:	Yes.

As shown in Extracts 3.14, 3.15 and 3.16, the workgroup actively prevented defendants from speaking freely. See, for example, the short one-word answer of the defence solicitor in Extract 3.16 or how the district judge shouts at the defendant in Extract 3.14. These interruptions denied defendants a voice in proceedings and, typically, defendants received such interruptions negatively (as seen in Extracts 3.14 and 3.15). Indeed, defendants appeared to be frustrated at not being able to contribute their voice to proceedings. It was the researchers view that staff acted in this controlling manner over defendants because they were primarily concerned with speedy justice ends.

Second, and in relation to the prior point, the court workgroup's quick processing of cases caused defendants to not understand proceedings. This point applies to summary justice proceedings generally, as well as those parts of the process that focus specifically on defendants. The following example extract demonstrates staff's prioritization of speed over defendant comprehension:

Extract 3.17

Legal advisor:	Please stand Mr Defendant … would you like your trial in this court or in the Crown Court?
Defendant:	Sorry I never understood that. *[The legal advisor reiterates the previous question, speaking very fast]*
Defence solicitor:	[Interrupts] He wishes it to be dealt with here.

In Extract 3.17, court staff seemed aware that the defendant did not understand what was being asked of them. Instead of the court workgroup focusing on the defendant's capacity to comprehend the question and have them contribute, the legal advisor repeats the misunderstood question at speed and then the solicitor interjects. Here, the court workgroup effectively omits the defendant's role in the summary justice process. In this way, the court workgroup worked together, upholding the shared value of speedy justice by managing defendants' participation in proceedings.

In further support of this point, staff would often refuse to provide defendants with a written summary of their hearing, which allowed staff to dispose of cases more quickly. Defendants' requests for a written summary seemed to emanate from their lack of comprehension of the court process. Consider Extracts 3.18 and 3.19 that support this point:

Extract 3.18

Magistrate:	We are adjourning onto the x date.
Defendant:	Erm. Can you put that in writing? I've got my address … [Speech trails off]

Legal advisor:	No, we won't do that, you are here in court so now the onus is on you.

Extract 3.19

District judge:	I am going to extend the drug rehabilitation order until x date/time, this year. You will also have another appearance here at the court for review on the x date/time.
Defendant:	Please, can someone write all this down for me. I have, I have …
Defence solicitor:	Don't worry Ms Defendant, I will get this to you.

In Extract 3.18, the defendant requested assistance in order to comprehend what the justice process expected of them following the hearing (possibly such as when they were to attend the next hearing). Despite this, the legal advisor refused to assist the defendant. This likely caused the defendant to leave the courthouse with only a partial understanding of the hearing they attended. The researcher interpreted that staff did not intend to confuse defendants, as suggested with the defence solicitor's comments in Extract 3.19. In this extract, the solicitor did not write down anything for their client in-court but they did have a conversation when courtroom proceedings concluded. In both example extracts, staff were primarily concerned with achieving speedy case disposals during the in-court summary justice process.

Third, legal advisors would mute defendants during live link hearings to prevent them from interrupting the summary justice process. Indeed, during the data collection period, legal advisors would regularly mute a defendant during their hearing without the consent of the defendant and without forewarning. The result was that cases would go uninterrupted by the defendant and, therefore, the workgroup could dispose of cases quickly. Consider Extract 3.20, which demonstrates a legal advisor muting a defendant for 45 minutes during a bail hearing:

Extract 3.20

Legal advisor:	[Picks up TV/live link remote and unmutes video link screen] Alright Mr Live Link officer, can you hear us again?
Live link officer:	Hello, yes, I do.
Legal advisor:	Could you please bring us Mr Defendant?
Live link officer:	Yes, I will do now.
	[Time elapses. The defendant enters on the TV/live link screen]
Legal advisor:	Right, okay. Mr Defendant, can you hear us okay?
Defendant:	Yeah, fine thanks.
Legal advisor:	[Legal advisor conducts identification checks with the defendant] Okay, so I see here you have appeared before the court on x date, the case was, erm. Sorry, a not guilty plea was given with a trial date fixed on the x date, do you remain not guilty?
Defendant:	Yes.
Legal advisor:	Okay, just listen carefully please. [The legal advisor mutes the defendant via a remote control]
	[The prosecution solicitor presents a case for no bail. This is followed by the defence solicitor who presents a case for bail. Approximately 45 minutes elapse during this period]
Magistrate:	Yes, I don't know if you heard that [now talking to the defendant onscreen], but there will be another video link hearing.
	[Legal advisor unmutes the defendant]
Defendant:	Yep.
Magistrate:	Alright Thank you.
	[End of hearing]

In Extract 3.20, the observed muting of defendants for significant periods of time was typical of how legal advisors controlled defendants during live link hearings. Legal advisors would unmute a defendant only when a crucial information exchange was necessary, such as when they asked for a defendant's confirmation of plea. Legal advisors only unmuted defendants for key information exchanges, reflecting their prioritization of speedy justice.

Fourth, the court workgroup would rely on defendants as being an in-court source of information regarding their means, so as to streamline the case disposal process. Means information was important during sentencing hearings as this allowed magistrates and district judges to deliver proportionate sanctions. Indeed, it allowed sentencers to deliver a financial punishment (fine, compensation order, and so on) that was based on the defendant's unique financial circumstances. In the observed data, however, it was common practice for defendants to express that they were not sure of the accuracy of the means information they were providing to court staff. Regardless, court staff would accept this potential error by requesting that the defendant provide information to the best of their ability. Following this, the magistrates or district judge would immediately sentence the defendant. This practice almost certainly undercut the proportionality purpose of financial means forms.

Extract 3.21

Magistrate:	You know you don't need exact figures, just whatever is fine; just fill in the boxes. Don't bother with everything like 'catalogues' and whatever. [Referring to the financial means form the defendant is completing in the courtroom]
Defendant:	Sure, sure.

	[Silence. Time elapses as the defendant continues to complete the means form. The court usher exits the courtroom via the public entrance. Silence continues]
Magistrate:	Are you there?
Defendant:	Well, the best I can, off the top of my head.
Magistrate:	[Interrupts] Don't worry, don't worry! Well, we will now retire and consider this. *[The court usher hands over the now completed financial means form from the defendant to the magistrate]*
Defence solicitor:	[Murmurs/whispers to the defendant] Don't be alarmed about that, that is normal.

As demonstrated in Extract 3.21, the defendant was not prepared to provide an accurate statement of means to the court. Regardless, staff encouraged the defendant to present the information, which resulted in the case being finalized quickly. A court usher succinctly identified this problem early in the data collection process when they commented, 'There is no way to tell if what they [defendants] put on the means form is true, we just have to believe them'.[1] Despite questions of information accuracy being raised here, the researcher interpreted this defendant management practice of staff as being primarily for speedy justice.

Finally, as a caveat to the prior points, the researcher observed that court hearings would slow down in pace if a defendant represented themselves during a hearing (that is, if a defendant engaged in 'DIY defence'[2]). The following example extracts serve to demonstrate how proceedings would slow down during such DIY defence cases. For greater context, Extract 3.22 is from an exceptional hardship hearing[3] which the defendant, after attending the hearing, realized that the procedure was not something they wanted to pursue. Meanwhile, in Extract 3.23, the magistrate engages in a lengthy conversation to ensure the defendant understands the impositions that the court has made against them. Both example cases draw attention to how a lack of representation slows down the summary justice process.

Extract 3.22

Legal advisor:	Mr Defendant entered an early guilty plea on the x date, it is before you today … the speed appears to be 52 mph in a 40 mph limit, erm [pause] … is there anything you wish to tell the magistrates about in relation to the offence here today Mr Defendant?
Defendant:	Nothing.
Legal advisor:	Nothing? Okay … so your driving record has 9 points on it … there are three other convictions on here … the magistrates must consider disqualification for at least 6 months unless you can demonstrate to the magistrates you will suffer exceptional hardship. Do you have any evidence with you today?
Defendant:	No, I don't … the first thing is, that, I take responsibility … I take responsibility for taking the children to school …
Magistrate:	[Interrupts] You must remember that this isn't 'ordinary hardship', this must be 'exceptional hardship'.
Defendant:	Well, I have no basis. I am sorry that I have wasted your time, erm.

Extract 3.23

Magistrate:	You came here today to do a statutory declaration and you don't even have that

	[referring to evidence to support the statutory declaration], from the post office?
Defendant:	Well, I never knew what this was today. I have had so many court hearings that …
Magistrate:	No, no, you should have brought your evidence with you today. Do you understand the predicament here today?
Defendant:	Well, sorry. When I spoke to the lady downstairs, she just said I should turn up and talk to the magistrates and speak to the magistrates and that would be that.
Magistrate:	Well, yeah, you can present your case, but you need evidence. *[Time elapses as the magistrate and defendant attempt to clarify the impositions the court has made against the defendant]*

Extracts 3.22 and 3.23 serve to demonstrate how key procedural issues became problems when a defendant represented themselves during a hearing. Either hearings were listed that did not need to take place (as with Extract 3.22) or a significant portion of time was spent explaining to defendants the details of procedure and their importance (as with Extract 3.23). This final observation serves as a caveat to the prior points because in such DIY cases the court workgroup would slow down proceedings as key procedural steps rested on the actions of defendants. Indeed, the court workgroup was limited in such cases to manage defendants for speedy justice ends.

3.5 Summary

This chapter has argued that during the observation period, the value of speed-focused managerialism characterized the lower criminal court process. Namely, district judges promoted speediness through controlling conversational turn-taking among staff and court users, by adopting an intimidating character and by actively discouraging court staff from upholding any other values that were not for speediness. Meanwhile, magistrates made frequent use of retirements to enable a cooperative, speed-focused space to emerge for legal advisors and solicitors. At the same time, solicitors upheld speed-focused managerialism by working together (typically in pairs) in the short time before a formal hearing was scheduled to take place. Here, they would resolve otherwise time-consuming case management issues as well as determine hearing/case outcomes in advance. Additionally, prosecution solicitors would rarely contest defendants' mitigating factors, further speeding up the case disposal process. In further support for this chapter's central argument, court staff would control conversational turn-taking regarding defendants to resolve cases quickly, seemingly to the detriment of defendants' ability to understand proceedings. In further controlling conversational turn-taking, legal advisors would mute defendants for prolonged periods during live link hearings (preventing them from interrupting and slowing down the justice process). The court workgroup would also rely on a defendant as a convenient in-court information source, so that they could expediently address questions regarding the defendant's financial means (which raised information accuracy concerns).

This chapter has also drawn attention to two caveat points, emphasizing where the summary justice process did not uphold the value of speed-focused managerialism. Namely, during the cross-examination portion of trials, solicitors would not prioritize speediness. Instead, solicitors prioritized traditional adversarialism. Meanwhile, defendants' DIY defence practices limited the court workgroups' capacity to manage defendants for speedy justice ends. Indeed, defendants' inability to fully understand and therefore engage with legal proceedings slowed down the justice process.

Section 6.2 offers a critical discussion that builds from the observations of the present chapter. This latter section discusses how the observed speed-focused managerial practices are for over-efficiency, eroding the quality of the justice process.

FOUR

Standardized Defendant Processes

4.1 Introduction

This chapter presents the second of three key themes that the researcher identified from their observations of the summary justice process. This key theme (or overarching value) is, 'standardized defendant processes'. The present chapter explains how staff and institutional-level practices upheld the value of standardization by processing all defendants in a similar manner, despite there being significant differences between defendants. This chapter explains these standardized processes by unpacking three subthemes: underused defendant mental health diversion processes (see Section 4.2), under-specialized processes for substance-related offenders (see Section 4.3) and finally, absent multiple disadvantage-addressing processes (see Section 4.4). As in the prior chapter, these subthemes draw upon example extracts throughout to evidence the researcher's interpretation of the data. By following this method, this chapter demonstrates how the researcher formed the subthemes, and how these subthemes support the chapter's overarching theme. In Chapter 6, Section 6.3 offers a critical analysis of the present chapter, arguing that such standardized defendant processes are problematically for over-efficiency and therefore, the lower criminal courts should welcome policy reform.

4.2 Underused mental health diversion processes

First, court staff would refrain from investigating in-court evidence of defendants' mental health disorders. Throughout the data collection period, the researcher observed several defendants that he suspected were living with a mental health-related issue which went unaddressed by the court workgroup during the in-court process. As Extract 4.1 demonstrates, these suspected defendants would display behaviour that was highly erratic, their behaviours would often be volatile and aggressive. Alternatively, as Extract 4.2 demonstrates, suspected mental health affected defendants would be intensely introverted and childlike.

Extract 4.1

	[The cells officer was halfway through taking off the defendant's handcuffs, then puts them back on the defendant. The defendant is arguing with cells officer in the dock. Details of this argument are inaudible]
Legal advisor:	Mr Defendant, could you give the court your full name?
Defendant:	I don't feel very well! I need my medication! Let me out! I need my medication!
District judge:	That will happen as soon as possible.
Defendant:	Let me get out, this is bullshit yo! Let me tell you then, I'm on recall, this is stupid, I'm ill.
District judge:	Please be quiet!

Extract 4.2

Legal advisor:	Do you have anything to add?
Defendant:	[Silent/no response]

Defence solicitor:	Well, I think he knows [shouting almost at their client, the defendant] that you have been very fairly treated today. And you are not, not, not going to be doing anything like that again, are you?
Defendant:	[Shakes head]
Magistrate:	So, do you have any help with, erm, at home?
Defendant:	No.
Magistrate:	And do you live with anyone?
Defendant:	[Shakes head]
Magistrate:	Right, well you need to appear at x court at x date.

Extracts 4.1 and 4.2 reveal common court workgroup practices: when a defendant presented behavioural evidence that they were living with a mental health issue(s) during proceedings, staff would refrain from investigating these issues. Instead, staff would commit to proceedings as normal. Consequently, it was unclear whether the defendant was of sound mind and, ultimately, whether the court workgroup should have diverted the defendant onto a mental health pathway. Indeed, in Extract 4.1, court staff dismissed the defendant's concerns regarding access to medication during in-court proceedings. Staff did not respond by investigating what the defendant meant by "I need my medication", or whether the defendants (mental) wellbeing was suffering. Similarly, staff in Extract 4.2 did not explore the defendant's mental wellbeing despite there being in-court, behavioural evidence from the defendant that they were living with a mental health vulnerability/disorder. The researcher took this interpretation owing to the childlike, meek behaviour of the defendant. Additionally, court staff spoke to the defendant in very simplified English and in a manner that suggested that they were aware that the defendant was living with a mental health issue. Despite this evidence, the process continued in a similar

fashion to other hearings, without an in-court investigation into the wellbeing of the defendant.

Second, magistrates and judges often assumed a position of disbelief regarding the claimed mental health issues of defendants. Extracts 4.3 and 4.4 demonstrate this position. In Extract 4.3, the defence solicitor attempts to bring to the attention of the court that their client has a mental health diagnosis, and potentially, therefore, the court should divert their client onto a mental health pathway. Meanwhile, Extract 4.4 demonstrates the disbelief from one magistrate in the brief time between court hearings, when the defendant was absent from court.

Extract 4.3

District judge:	Time and again I hear that 'he has mental health issues', he only has mental health issues unless he has been diagnosed.
Defence solicitor:	Well, I have a letter here from his doctor here saying that he has ongoing mental struggles.
District judge:	What does that mean? Has he been to see a psychiatrist? Has he a condition?
Defence solicitor:	Erm, well ... [Gestures to papers/shows document]
District judge:	I'll read it! Pass it here! [The district judge is almost shouting. Usher passes document from the solicitor to the judge]

Extract 4.4

	[The defendant leaves the courtroom]
Magistrate #1:	Well. He will be going to jail.
Magistrate #2:	Yeah. Yeah. Yeah, mental health pffft!

As Extracts 4.3 and 4.4 demonstrate, both district judges and magistrates assumed a position of disbelief when being informed of a defendant's adverse mental health condition. Furthermore, when written evidence was available to support a claim that a defendant was living with a mental health issue (which could warrant diversion) this seemed to annoy court staff. Indeed, this was the interpretation of the researcher regarding Extract 4.3, where the judge appeared to be aggravated by the availability of such evidence. To this end, the researcher interpreted district judges and magistrates as being committed to processing all defendants in a standardized manner, accepting a default position of disbelief if a defendant claimed that they had mental health issues.

Third, staff were unfamiliar with how to action mental health diversion processes. Extract 4.5 demonstrates this. Here, a solicitor makes a district judge aware of a defendant's poor mental health and following this, the district judge asks the workgroup for confirmation as how to proceed. This suggests the district judge was unfamiliar with non-standardized processes:

Extract 4.5

Defence solicitor:	He [the defendant] is clearly, clearly unwell ... I am aware that he faces a very real risk that he will return to prison today.
District judge:	And he is, erm, very unwell?
Defence solicitor:	I believe that if we take this, him, out of the system, that is undoubtably; that would be the best way forward.
District judge:	Who makes that decision?
Defence solicitor:	My friend here.
District judge:	The Crown? [Referring to the prosecution solicitor]
Defence solicitor:	The Crown.
District judge:	Okay, so the reality is that he needs mental health services ... so how does this work? Detain him under the Mental Health Act?

In this example extract, the district judge demonstrates that they are unfamiliar with how to action the mental health diversion process. Indeed, they ask for confirmation from hierarchically, lower-ranking members of the court workgroup regarding how to proceed. Consequently, the researcher took the view that the district judge embodied the value of procedural standardization because of their unfamiliarity with the diversion pathway.

4.3 Under-specialized processes for substance-related offending

First, under no circumstances did sentencers (district judges and magistrates) accept substance-compelled explanations of behaviour as a mitigating factor. Contrary to framing substance use as a defence or mitigating factor, solicitors framed substance use as a criminal offence or as an aggravating factor. This meant that sentencers would increase the severity of sanctions when an offender was under the influence of a substance. In Extract 4.6, a brief statement from a district judge demonstrates this institutional practice:

Extract 4.6

District judge: Please stand Mr Defendant … you say that you were drinking and on drugs and you present that as a mitigating factor, it's not, it's an aggravating factor.

The framing of substance use as an aggravating factor characterizes the offender as being irresponsible. This is an institutional practice not only because the researcher widely observed statements such as this from sentencers, but also because the Sentencing Council's (2004) guidelines regarding what qualifies as mitigating and aggravating factors establishes this position formally. This acceptance of substance use as an aggravating factor functions when a presumption is made that the offender has voluntary control regarding whether they consume a given substance or not. Often, however, solicitors and probation officers would report that defendants/offenders were under the addictive influence of a substance, revoking their voluntary control and therefore, at least to some degree, the defendant's culpability was lessened. This raises jurisprudence concerns regarding the myopic, standardized view of the summary justice process when sentencing substance-related offenders.

Indeed, substance-addiction cases raised unique jurisprudence questions about whether it was appropriate for the court to punish such offenders more harshly than non-substance-addicted offenders. Often the court seemed to accept that an offender's criminal action was due in part to the offender's substance addiction and, at the same time, these offenders would also often express that they did not want to be addicted. Consequently, the offender's culpability was in question: the offender's voluntary control over their (criminal) behaviour was apparently diminished, and yet the courts punished these offenders more severely than other similar non-addicted, non-substance-using offenders whose voluntary control over their behaviour was not in doubt. Consider the following example extracts that draw attention to this jurisprudence issue regarding substance-related sentencing hearings.[1] In Extract 4.7, the offender is being sentenced for the offence of criminal damage. Meanwhile, in Extract 4.8, the offender is being sentenced for theft. In both of these extracts, the offender's substance use was framed as being an addiction.

Extract 4.7

Defence solicitor: The problems that Mr Defendant has had recently, has been mainly due to

	a spice addiction. [The defendant/offender is crying] He is really struggling to overcome that particular addiction ... with regards to the cell damage, he defecated in the cell and wiped the contents around the cell and it had to be subsequently cleaned. He does say, however, that at the time he was in a bad place and he apologises profusely. *[Time elapses]*
Magistrate:	Right, Mr Defendant. Is there anything you wish to add?
Defendant:	... I am so sorry for causing the commotion and erm, I wasn't erm [the defendant is crying, unable to speak] ... I am so sorry, I have never done anything like this. [Defendant cries/sobs uncontrollably]

Extract 4.8

Probation officer:	Good morning ma'am, this is the 6 shop thefts, the background is that he has a drug addiction ... of note is that he has been abstinent until 8 months ago ... he was using about £20 of heroin and £20 of crack cocaine which was being funded for by his crimes ... he sees being caught a something of a blessing ... he says now that he wants to go back to his AA meetings.

In the researcher's interpretation, such offenders sincerely desired to be addiction-free. In Extract 4.7, the offenders appeared to be genuinely remorseful for their substance-related offending (the criminal damage to the cell). Meanwhile, in Extract 4.8, the offender reported that their current involvement with the justice system, 'being caught', was a 'blessing' because it provided access to an alcohol recovery programme. These unique displays of addicted offenders expressing remorse and claiming a desire to be addiction-free brings into question the culpability of offenders. Indeed, there is evidence to suggest that their actions were, at least in part, compelled by their unwanted addictions to substances. Consequently, there is reason to frame such offenders as being of lesser culpability than non-addicted individuals, which would also mean that these individuals would warrant mitigated (not aggravated) sentences. Despite this, individuals who identified as being addicted to a substance were processed in a standardized manner. To reiterate, under no circumstances were addiction-based explanations accepted by the court as a mitigating factor; the courts always framed substance use as an aggravating factor.

Second, sentencers morally reprimanded substance-related offenders like non-substance-related offenders. It was common throughout the observation period for the bench to explore an offender's substance abuse by questioning them. In doing so, like with other non-substance-related sentencing hearings, the bench would morally reprimand the offender's behaviour before formally sentencing them. The following extracts exemplify such moral reprimands:

Extract 4.9

Magistrate:	I think you have a problem with drink.
Defendant:	[Strong Eastern European accent] Well, I, I did not drink all of last year then I did at December.
Magistrate:	... what do you drink?
Defendant:	Vodka, beer and cider.
Magistrate:	Not very healthy, is it?

Defendant: Erm, sorry?
Magistrate: I said, that's not very healthy. Is it?
Defendant: Erm, no.
Magistrate: And what do you intend to try and do with yourself?
Defendant: I have an … [Inaudible]
Magistrate: I can't understand you. Speak up. And slowly.
Defendant: I, I, I have an appointment [pause] with the alcohol team and erm, they are to treat me for erm, [pause] alcohol.

Extract 4.10

Magistrate: How much do you usually pay per, erm, portion [cocaine]?
Defendant: Too much, too much. I am hoping to get help from probation.
Magistrate: How much per hit?
Defendant: About 20.
Magistrate: That's a lot, isn't it?
Defendant: Yeah, too much.
Magistrate: … you are wasting your money away, aren't you? Not good, is it?

In the Extracts 4.9 and 4.10, it is the researcher's interpretation that the magistrates framed the offenders' substance abuse behaviour as morally reprehensible, as they regard it as being part of a lifestyle that is within the offenders' control. In Extract 4.9, the magistrates framed the offender's substance abuse as being akin to a lack of self-care and self-entrepreneurship: "Not very healthy is it?", "what do you intend to try and do with yourself?" Similarly, in Extract 4.10, the magistrate framed the offender's spending on substances as representative of poor individual choice: "you are wasting your money away aren't you? Not good, is it?" Such comments from the bench on moral behaviour and lifestyle choice were common throughout all sentencing hearings. For example, it was typical of the bench to scold traffic offenders for having a history of speeding. To this end, sentencers' indiscriminate moral reprimanding behaviour represented a commitment to the value of procedural standardization.

Third, and connecting from the previous point regarding sentencers' moral reprimands, sentencers responsibilized substance-related offenders like non-substance-related offenders. Indeed, the responsibilization aspect of sentencing hearings would follow the benches moral reprimands. In this way, sentencing hearings were logical: once sentencers established an offender's morally poor behaviour, defendants were then told to take on greater responsibility so as to change in some manner. The following example extracts demonstrate this responsibilization aspect of the summary justice process. In both of the following example extracts, the defence has made clear to the court that the defendant was addicted to a substance and this was a factor at the time of their offending. Regardless, district judges and magistrates would typically insist that substance-related offenders take greater responsibility for their circumstances, as was normal practice for non-substance-related offending.

Extract 4.11

District judge:	Please stand Ms Defendant. I understand that your life has been chaotic ... still [pause] if anyone is to signpost you or to help you it is your offender manager ... the probation service is willing to work with you again. If you have any further breaches ... you are likely to have this order revoked and you will likely go to prison, do you understand that?
Defendant:	Yes, yes. [Crying]

Extract 4.12

Magistrate: ... [if] you commit any other offence again in the next 9 months then you will be brought back to the court to deal with this matter ... you must make sure that you take responsibility for this imposition and make sure its paid do you understand?

Defendant: Yes, sir.

Indeed, Extracts 4.11 and 4.12 demonstrate how district judges and magistrates would regularly responsibilize substance-related offenders, encouraging them to better engage with criminal justice services, to adhere by their criminal sentence and to resolve their substance addictions. Like with the previous point regarding culpability and jurisprudence, the bench would not explore the link between substance addiction and self-control. Therefore, the capacity of substance-related offenders to take on any responsibility successfully was unknown. Such a consideration was understandably not present with other offence types, such as that of traffic offending, as the capacity to exercise self-control was not in doubt. However, the fact that such offenders often had lifelong connections to substance abuse (as discussed throughout this section) brings into doubt their capacity to exercise self-control and, therefore, abide by their sentence, which includes attending probation-related events and paying impositions on time. Despite this uniqueness regarding substance-related offending, sentencers responsibilized all offenders in a standardized manner.

Finally, this section offers a fourth point which is a caveat to the previous three points. The researcher interpreted the observed drug rehabilitation requirement[2] (DRR) hearings as prioritizing the values of personableness and problem-solving. However, the observed courthouse rarely practised these DRR hearings and, in the researcher's interpretation, the processes were not specialized enough to substantially address the concerns raised by the substance-related offenders. Consequently, the overarching subtheme (standardization) remains despite this caveat. The following extracts unpack how DRR courts were different from all other hearing types. Of note here, is the magistrates' tone in welcoming the offenders and how the offenders speak freely about the social obstacles they have been facing:

Extract 4.13

Magistrate: We have been going through this and its great [referring to the report in front of them]. Drug wise, are you on substitutes?
Defendant: Well. I am using.
Magistrate: You are?
Defendant: Yeah, I'm on cannabis but no longer on cocaine. And erm, I realized that alcohol really changes me, so that's why I fell into erm, smoking a bit more weed.
Magistrate: Right, what was that catalyst for all of this?
Defendant: Well. I would say it was the death of my cousin 5 years ago, so, erm, yeah.

Extract 4.14

Magistrate: Hiya, hello, do we call you? X or X?
Defendant: X if you want
Magistrate: How are you doing X?
Defendant: I have a bit of a cold.
[Time elapses]
Magistrate: Right, so what's the problem?
Defendant: Just really depressed.
Magistrate: Right, have you been keeping your appointment with probation?

In Extracts 4.13 and 4.14, the offenders gave candid accounts of their disadvantaged (and criminal) lifestyles. This is evident in Extract 4.13 where the defendant explains that despite their previous substance-related criminal history, they have continued to take drugs. From this, the magistrates explored what specific factors related to the defendant's continued substance use, which was a family death. Similarly, in Extract 4.14, the magistrates began personably by asking the defendant, "How are you doing?" This sociable element is not typical of summary justice proceedings. Indeed, see Chapter 4, which discusses the theme of speediness. Following this, the magistrates openly asked the defendant what issues were affecting them (depression). In this way, the criminal justice process in these examples was something that the defendant was involved in, rather than the justice process being something that was done to them: defendants could freely explain the issues they were facing because of the non-standardized, slow pace of proceedings and the personableness of the magistrates.

Problematically, however, the present study observed that the advice offered by magistrates was amateur in nature and, consequently, magistrates' individual problem-solving during DRR hearings was not as substantive as it could have been. The following extract is a continuation of the hearing in Extract 4.13 and demonstrates the limits of magistrates' problem-solving advice. For greater context, the offender in Extracts 4.13 and 4.15 has a known history of substance abuse and, as discovered through the exploratory DRR court method, the offender's motivation for their criminal behaviour stems from unresolved trauma surrounding the death of their cousin. In view of this, the sitting magistrates offered the following advice:

Extract 4.15

Magistrate:	Very good, well I think you are on track. The drugs, the cannabis, is not good for you. I recommend that you stay away from it.

While this extract is brief, this is also the extent of the advice the magistrate offered the defendant. The magistrate's advice does embody a socially supportive quality, yet in the researcher's interpretation they do not adequately address the reason for the offenders reoccurring behaviour (the adverse psychological impact of the defendant's deceased cousin). Indeed, the advice of the magistrate appeals to the defendant's sense of self-control, as the magistrate urges the offender to "stay away from it [drugs]". In this way, magistrates' DRR hearings, like in other court hearings, embodied the same standardized approach of responsibilizing defendants for their criminal behaviour and life-style changes.

The researcher made a similar observation regarding the case in Extract 4.14, these magistrates also offered the defendant limited advice. To explain further, the offender in this case recounted that they lived with severe depression and, as a result, they lacked motivation: they felt like they "can't do anything at the moment". The defendant clarified that their depression immobilized them: "I just get lost in myself." Following this, the magistrate offered the following advice:

Extract 4.16

Magistrate:	Right, well, what you are going to do when you leave here? You will leave here and get a calendar, get a pen and write on it, colour code it!
Defendant:	Yeah, that's a good start.
Magistrate:	Isn't it!

Like in the previous example case (Extracts 4.13 and 4.15), the advice given by the magistrate in this case (Extracts 4.14 and 4.16) does not substantially engage with the underlying cause of the defendant's substance-related behaviour (their severe depression). Instead, the magistrate compels the defendant to "get a calendar, get a pen and write on it, colour code it". Again, the observed justice undercuts the hearing's problem-solving qualities by appealing to the defendant's sense of self-control (responsibilization), encouraging the defendant to overcome their adversity through self-organization. Therefore, to reiterate, the magistrates in DRR hearings embodied the same responsibilizing approach that was present in other non-DRR hearings. Responsibilizing defendants was a standardized process in the observed courthouse, regardless of whether defendants' crimes were substance-related or whether they engaged in DRR hearings.

4.4 Absent multiple disadvantage-addressing processes

It was common throughout the data collection period for defendants to embody multiple disadvantaging factors that intersected, creating unique compounded forms of disadvantage. In all three of the following example extracts, the defendants were reportedly homeless, dependent on drugs and/or alcohol (addicted) and had severe mental health issues. For greater context, in Extract 4.17, the police arrested and charged the defendant for possession of a bladed article. Meanwhile, in Extract 4.18, the defendant appeared at court for breach of a probation order (a substance-related rehabilitation activity requirement[3]). Finally, in Extract 4.19, the police had arrested and charged the defendant for stealing cash from a local shop.

Extract 4.17

Defence solicitor:	Could you please explain the nature of having the bladed article?
Defendant:	Well, I was upset at the time and I was intending to use the article to cause damage to myself and end my life.

Extract 4.18

Defence solicitor: Mr Defendant has not been paid any benefits since December last year because he doesn't have a bank account and he uses that account of his friend ... he is currently on anti-depressants medication ... he tells me he doesn't have a will to live ... he says that he begs every day and all day. He tells me that he does not actively beg but he just sits and waits because he doesn't want to get arrested for begging ... he tells me about his day to day living and he, he tells me first thing in the morning he throws up, he is not a very well man ... in these circumstances it is very hard for him to comply with services ...

Extract 4.19

Defence solicitor: The [stolen] money used was to take drugs, and purchase the hotel room. The rest of the money was recovered, and those drugs were to be used for an overdose ... so yes, this is a sad case your worships. This is not something that was done maliciously or vindictively, this is a sad case, he is simply unwell.

In all of the these examples, the researcher framed the issues of homelessness, drug use and poor mental health as disadvantaging factors because they reportedly related to the criminality of defendants/offenders. One form of disadvantage appeared to link in or explain in part other forms of disadvantage. Consider Extract 4.19, where the homeless defendant stole money to pay for hotel lodging and drugs in order to establish the conditions they felt were necessary to commit suicide. In terms of criminality, this defendants' case is characterized by a form of disadvantage that is significantly different to an offender who only stole money for drug use/to satiate an addiction. Indeed, the form of disadvantage here is compounded. This is similarly the case for the defendant in Extract 4.18. Here, the defendant's unique form of compounded disadvantage made it difficult for them to comply with social services, resulting in them breaching their court order. Meanwhile, the defendant in Extract 4.17 was in possession of a bladed article for the purpose of suicide. In this case, the defendants poor mental health was a causal factor for their offence (similarly reported in Extract 4.19).

Second, the observed courthouse processed and sentenced disadvantaged defendants/offenders the same as other non-disadvantaged defendants/offenders. This is despite the unique interplay that disadvantaging factors had in influencing offenders' behaviour. The following extracts show these standardized processes. For context, in Extract 4.20 the defendant was street homeless and faced the charge of stealing food (theft). Meanwhile, in Extract 4.21 the defendant was street homeless and faced the charge of possession of a bladed article (a knife):

Extract 4.20

District judge: You pleaded guilty to shop lifting that happened last year … at the time, I understand that you had to steal to buy food, regardless that doesn't make it acceptable.

Extract 4.21

Probation officer: He is currently living, for the majority of time, on the street … he says the knife is just for self-defence, being on the street he says he has been attacked a number of times and that is why he had it in his possession …

In Extract 4.20, the researcher interpreted the offender's behaviour as being sustenance based: they stole food to meet basic living needs while being street homeless. Meanwhile, in Extract 4.21, the researcher interpreted the offender's behaviour as being self-defence based. As the probation officer clarifies, the offender possessed a blade in order to protect themselves, which was reasonable given that they had "been attacked a number of times". In this manner, the researcher understood that, often, disadvantage in its compounded forms connected to criminality. Despite this, the observed summary justice process did not account and adjust for disadvantage. Rather, the court processed and sentenced disadvantaged offenders in a standardized manner, regardless of whether their criminality related to sustenance or personal protection concerns.

Third, and as a caveat to the previous observation, staff would vocalize their dissatisfaction with how the lower courts processed disadvantaged defendants/offenders, drawing attention to institutional constraints. The following example extract demonstrates this dissatisfaction of the court workgroup. For context, this extract captures the brief time between hearings when one defendant with compounded disadvantage left the courtroom and another defendant was brought in by an usher. This allowed the court workgroup to speak openly without a defendant being present.

Extract 4.22

	[Homeless defendant just left the courtroom]
Magistrate:	Accommodation is the key, isn't it? [Expressed enthusiastically]
Legal adviser:	Yeah.
Probation officer:	Yep.

Magistrate:	They have proved it, haven't they? I mean, that guy is absolutely, is totally ideal to be in housing, it would save on all other services if we could just get him in housing, reduce paramedic and other revolving door services!
Probation officer:	Yeah, yeah.

As demonstrated in this extract, while staff would formally uphold the value of standardization in the hearing process, once the hearing ended, court staff would sometimes voice dissatisfaction with the justice they delivered. This is evident in Extract 4.22, where the workgroup draws attention to how there is not enough housing support for homeless defendants and how this lack of support serves as a "revolving door" for other standardized criminal justice services. In doing so, staff demonstrated a professional appetite for a shift in institutional values away from standardization when it came to processing and sentencing disadvantaged defendants.

Fourth and finally, defence solicitors would argue for their client to receive lengthy prison sentences so that they could secure disadvantage-addressing programmes for their clients (defendants/offenders). Such programmes were otherwise not available through the standard court process. Indeed, at sentencing hearings, defence solicitors would often argue for their client to be imprisoned for lengthy periods of time, beyond what the prosecution solicitor would advocate for. In the researcher's interpretation, the reason for this was because defence solicitors believed that prisoners serving lengthy sentences gained access to robust interventionalist, problem-addressing programmes. Extract 4.23 evidences defence solicitors' pro-prison stance when representing defendants with multiple forms of disadvantage:

Extract 4.23

Defence solicitor:	No, sir, [my defendant has] no employment, bens [abbreviation for

> welfare benefits, such as Job Seekers Allowance] and no fixed abode … in my submission, in someone in my defendant's position, I would put before you in due course, it is impossible that he be stabilized, controlled or be shown how to comply with the community in a period of 14 days. If that was possible, then it would have worked when he was in custody in September, because he was returned on licence, so if the multi-agency approach that we hear about would have worked then, [he] would have been complying … the reason why he is not complying is because he has issues beyond his control … he has mental health issues beyond his control … he spent initially 3 months in custody, it is impossible to resolve or begin to resolve even in a 3-month period. It would have to be a longer project … a sentence of 6 years may well have assisted him. It may have … treated, medicated, and assisted him. I argue that a further 14-day period would do nothing. He will then be released and I am not a fortune reader but I imagine that he would still be in a position where he would not be able to comply … that is the harsh reality of his condition.

As the defence solicitor argues here, some of the observed defendants faced disadvantage that was "impossible to resolve or begin to resolve even in a 3-month period. It would have to be a longer project". Therefore, the defence solicitor seemingly found it reasonable to argue that their client should receive a long prison sentence because they believed this would give their client greater access to interventionist, problem-solving services. While the details of such disadvantage-addressing services remain unspecified, the defence solicitor maintains that a short "14 day [prison] period would do nothing", whereas "a sentence of 6 years may well have assisted him". It is notable that the defence solicitor made this recommendation for the defendant, who faced compounded disadvantage, in the belief that their unorthodox advisement was warranted, given the defendant's complex history. To this end, it was the researcher's interpretation that defence solicitors were against standardized institutional practices for defendants with complex and compounded forms of disadvantage.

4.5 Summary

In summary, this chapter has argued that the value of 'standardized defendant processes' characterized the lower criminal courts. In greater detail, this chapter has argued that court staff would avoid investigating defendants' mental health when there was in-court evidence to warrant such an investigation. Instead, court staff would maintain processing such defendants in a routine manner. At the same time, staff would often express disbelief regarding a defendant's alleged poor mental health, demonstrating a commitment to uniformly processing defendants. Additionally, evidence demonstrates that court staff were unfamiliar with how to action specialist diversion processes for mental health-affected defendants. Meanwhile, during the observation period, there were no instances where sentencers accepted substance-compelled explanations of behaviour as a mitigating factor; drawing attention to the rigidity of the summary justice process. This approach to justice delivery was despite defendants apparently sincere (and emotional) claims to not wanting to be addicted to various substances. Such offenders also expressed, again, seemingly sincerely, remorse and shame for their criminal behaviour while they were under the influence of substances. Contrary to viewing addiction as compelling behaviour, sentencers took it upon themselves to morally reprimand substance-related offenders, telling them to take greater responsibility for their actions. This moral reprimanding approach was typical across all criminal cases, substance related or not, further illustrating how the lower criminal courts were committed to standardized practices. Lastly, this chapter has argued that while the courts would often process defendants with multiple, compounded forms of disadvantage (namely homelessness, substance addiction and mental health issues), meaningful processes to address intersecting forms of disadvantage were lacking. Indeed, sentencers would process such defendants in a similar manner to defendants without multiple forms of disadvantage by telling them to take greater responsibility for their behaviour.

This chapter also raised a number of caveats and vignettes to enhance the richness of its findings. First, this chapter drew attention to how some sentencers expressed a desire to offer multiple-disadvantage-affected defendants with social housing in an effort to more effectively address their offending behaviour. This appeared paradoxical because moments before making such comments sentencers morally reprimanded/ responsibilized such individuals, suggesting that they believed that such offenders were sufficiently able to cease committing further criminal actions (such as drug use) without additional specialized interventions. This chapter also commented upon how the observed lower criminal courthouse made use of drug rehabilitation requirement hearings. These courts were able to comment upon some pressing social disadvantage issues that related to the offenders' criminal behaviour, but the magistrates were seemingly unable to offer meaningful, problem-solving advice. Additionally, such hearings were infrequent. As a result, the present chapter was able to defend its claim that the courts were characterized by the value 'standardized defendant processes'. Lastly, this chapter commented upon how defence solicitors would argue for their client to receive lengthy prison sentences so that they could secure disadvantage-addressing programmes. Indeed, defence solicitors appeared to believe that prison was a rehabilitative place and, therefore, for an offender characterized by multiple forms of disadvantage, was not a punishment that should be zealously contested. Rather, as illustrated with the observation data in this chapter, defence solicitors framed a lengthy prison sentence for such clients as a desirable outcome – sometimes arguing against the prosecution so that their client would receive a longer (rather than shorter) custodial sentence. In the researcher's interpretation, this demonstrated solicitors' dissatisfaction with the standardized justice process, suggesting that more specialized interventionist criminal justice would be welcomed.

Section 6.3 advances the initial data analysis presented in the present chapter. In doing so, Section 6.3 discusses how the observed standardized defendant processes contribute to the problem of over-efficiency, eroding the quality of the summary justice process.

FIVE

Court Users' Procedural Adversity

5.1 Introduction

This is the final findings chapter, focusing on the key theme (or overarching value), 'court users' procedural adversity'. Following the same method of the prior two chapters, this chapter draws upon example extracts from the observation period to illustrate how court users (defendants, witnesses and victims) engaged with summary justice processes that were demanding in some capacity. This chapter supports its final thematic claim by drawing upon two subthemes, 'adversity from oral evidence procedures' and 'adverse externalities for defendants'. In greater detail, Section 5.2 demonstrates how oral evidence procedures were emotionally demanding for victims/complainants, witnesses and defendants. Meanwhile, Section 5.3 discusses how issues such as travel costs and missed work opportunities had a negative impact on court users. Together, these two supporting subthemes illustrate some of the common experiences of court users that came to define the researcher's observations of the summary justice process. Chapter 6 offers a critical analysis of this key theme (or overarching value), arguing how such adversity is a form of inefficiency that has been overlooked by prior policy reform makers.

5.2 Adversity from oral evidence procedures

First, victims who gave oral evidence-in-chief experienced adversity when narrating the crime in question. The following example (Extract 5.1) demonstrates this point. For greater context, the victim/witness here is a non-native English speaker (which explains their improper use of English). The victim also gave this oral evidence prior to cross-examination (as is the case with oral evidence-in-chief), meaning that the victim/witness at this point was fresh to the day's in-court proceedings.

Extract 5.1

Prosecution solicitor:	What effect did it have on your mind, how did you feel?
Victim:	I will be crying lots of time, most of the times.
Prosecution solicitor:	How did you feel inside?
Victim:	I was feeling very bad.
Prosecution solicitor:	What specifically was it that made you feel bad?
Victim:	[Crying] I will think that I had been very, very good to him and he is still doing this to me.

In this example extract, the victim is evidently emotionally engaged. The process is, somewhat self-evidently, a negative emotional experience as the victim is crying during the process (despite the victim's solicitor leading proceedings). The researcher interpreted the adversity experienced by the victim as being connected to how their solicitor compelled them to narrate the effects of the crime: "What specifically was it that made you feel bad?" Rephrased, the oral evidence-in-chief process effectively caused the victim to relive the adverse emotional experience of the crime.

Second, solicitors' use of cross-examination often entwined emotionally intense accusations of disbelief. In greater detail, when solicitors were cross-examining a victim/complainant, they were often not emotionally sterile or forensic in their line of questioning. Rather, solicitors would entwine emotional force behind points of investigation. The following example extracts taken from cross-examinations supports this point:

Extract 5.2

Defence solicitor: Right, just to go back … he grabs the hand to which the scissors are in, do you remember that? And then he tries to bite your face, how does he do that? [The solicitor picks up and drops their stack of papers on the desk and looks at the witness]
Victim/complainant: I don't remember.
Defence solicitor: Wow. Wow. Well, you seemed very clear before didn't you? When my friend [referring to the prosecution solicitor] was talking to you.
Victim/complainant: [Interrupts/inaudible]
Defence solicitor: [Interrupts] Let me finish, please! [pause] So … there is a lot you can't remember, you can't remember a lot, isn't there?

Extract 5.3

Defence solicitor: You hid them [the defendants clothing] in a bag under the baby's pram, didn't you?
Victim/complainant: No, they were in plain sight.
Defence solicitor: [Cough-laughs] Alright. Huh, moving on.
…
Defence solicitor: [Interrupts] Well you never mentioned in your statement that you were slapped by Mr Defendant and that you were holding your

baby at the time? [Shouting, has a tone as if directed at a misbehaving child] I'm going to suggest that you never reported those things now did you because it simply didn't happen, did it! [pause] So. [pause] [lower tone, almost a whisper] Then what happened?

In Extract 5.2, and in the researcher's interpretation, when the solicitor interrupted the victim/complainant, this demonstrated/re-established a controlling power dynamic between the solicitor and the victim/complainant (similarly described in Section 3.4 with solicitor–defendant interactions). Additionally, in this same extract, the solicitor accentuated their disbelief regarding the victim's/complainant's account by dropping their stack of papers on their bench. Combining this power dynamic element with the solicitor's demonstration of disbelief gave the cross-examination process an emotionally intense character. Meanwhile, in Extract 5.3, the tone of the solicitor is also used to emphasize disbelief; the solicitor switches from shouting to quiet speaking. In the researcher's interpretation, this change in tone moved beyond the sterile cross-examination of facts and instead gave the courtroom atmosphere an emotionally hostile character. Indeed, for this reason, the researcher interpreted the cross-examination process for court users as an emotionally adverse one.

Third and finally, the cross-examination process also caused adversity specifically because it compelled court users to recount and explain issues of an intimate/sensitive nature. The following example extract demonstrates the often sensitive nature of such oral examinations. For context, this example draws upon the cross-examination of an elderly defendant who was charged with a motoring offence (speeding). The defendant also had a prior medical history of incontinence.

Extract 5.4

Prosecution solicitor:	What precautions do you usually take?
Defendant:	What do you mean? [Inaudible]
Prosecution solicitor:	What precautions do you take to prevent soiling yourself?
Defendant:	Well, there is nothing you can really do. It's just a sudden thing.
Prosecution solicitor:	Is there any sort of medical underwear that you can use?
Defendant:	Well, apart from wearing a nappy there is nothing I can do. Apart from wear a nappy, which is what I would use when I was in intensive care ... some days you can live with it and predict it, other days you cannot, it's very up and down.

This example extract is pertinent because it demonstrates the range of issues that affected court users. By solicitors testing the oral evidence of a witness, they would often scrutinize their sexual history, personal habits, and (as in Extract 5.4) medical history. Combined with solicitors' aforementioned emotional accusations of disbelief, solicitors' scrutiny of sensitive issues (such as a defendant's medical history) further rendered the summary justice process adverse for court users. This example is also pertinent as it draws attention to how the cross-examination process was emotionally adverse for both defendants and victims/complainants.

5.3 Adverse externalities for defendants

First, defendants would have to travel significant distances to attend court hearings. The following extract exemplifies this point. Here, the magistrate speaks to their legal advisor in the brief time between sentencing hearings for rail fare-related offences:

Extract 5.5

Magistrate:	Can I ask a question? [directed at the legal advisor] So, a lot of these travelling offences are between x city (~20–30 miles away) and x city (another city ~20–30 miles away). So, why are they coming here? Look at this defendant for example [gestures to papers], he lives in x city (~50 miles away).
Legal advisor:	I am not too sure, ma'am. It must have cost him a lot just to come here though.

Of note in Extract 5.5 is the fact that the members of the court workgroup seemed to be aware of the negative impact of non-local justice on defendants. Indeed, the cost of paying for a journey to attend a criminal hearing ~50 miles away for a non-serious criminal matter (non-payment of a train ticket in this case) would likely be equivalent to, or more costly than, the criminal fine/imposition made by the courts. This is, of course, presuming that the defendant would be found guilty of the offence. In cases where the court finds non-local defendants not guilty, the summary justice process effectively externalizes the cost of due process onto defendants. In this case, court users must endure the inconvenience of travel, including its financial cost, to establish their innocence. To this end, the researcher interpreted the institutional practice of listing cases in a non-local manner as embodying the value of extra-judicial adversity, because of its inconvenience-impact on defendants.

Second, some defendants reportedly experienced adversity because they had to forgo paid work in order to attend court hearings (and the courts did not compensate this missed paid work). Indeed, defendants often reported that they forwent paid work to attend court. The judiciary does not consider this externality (missed paid work) when attempting to form a proportionate sentence and there is no procedural means available for defendants to seek missed work compensation through central funds (see the Prosecution of Offenders Act 1985, s.4.4.1). Therefore, the summary justice process had an adverse effect on some defendants. Consider the following example extract which demonstrates the typical negative experience of defendants who have to miss paid work:

Extract 5.6

Magistrate:	I hope you realize that this is a matter that is something you should deal with directly.
Defendant:	Yeah, I feel it. I lost work of over £1,000 just to be here.
Magistrate:	Very well, you may leave.

Of course, the researcher could not verify the statement from the defendant as being factually true owing to the limitations of the present study's observation-only method. The present study did not investigate whether the defendant in Extract 5.6 actually forwent £1,000 worth of paid work in order to attend court. Still, the present study emphasizes that this sentiment was common throughout the collected data: defendants regularly voiced concern in-court that they had incurred financial losses because their court attendance resulted in missed paid work. Owing to the frequency at which defendants raised similar concerns, the researcher believes it likely that defendants did incur a punishing effect because of missed paid work opportunities, although the exact financial amount is unknown. Again, therefore, the researcher interpreted the observed summary justice as embodying the value of procedural adversity: defendants experienced adversity (missed paid work) from participating in the summary justice process.

Third, when the court held defendants in remand, defendants found this an emotionally demanding experience. To reiterate briefly from Chapter 2, remand is when criminal justice authorities (typically a local courthouse or prison) hold a defendant in custody while they await trial. The following example extracts demonstrate this emotionally challenging experience for defendants. For context, Extract 5.7 is from a sentencing hearing. Meanwhile, Extract 5.8 shows a defence solicitor speaking to a prosecution solicitor in between hearings. In this latter extract, the defence solicitor had just returned from the courthouse cells where his client was reportedly agitated by his confined space.

Extract 5.7

Defence solicitor:	You have already heard that Mr Defendant has no previous convictions ... he has spent the night in the cells ... [murmurs/whispers to the defendant] [Pauses] My client tells me that being in custody is 'the worst time of his life'.

Extract 5.8

Defence solicitor:	I knew this would happen, he [the defendant] is just getting aggressive because he is locked up there. This is what happened yesterday.

In both example extracts, the defendants had negative experiences of remand. Throughout the data collection period, the researcher observed that remanded defendants spent varying amounts of time in custody (whether a few days, as with Extract 5.7, or a few weeks, as in Extract 5.8). While the researcher recognizes that time spent in remand was often used to off-set criminal sentences, on other occasions defendants were not found guilty of a crime. To rephrase, sometimes defendants would spend significant periods of time (whether days or weeks) in remand (a cell), without being guilty of a crime. It is the researcher's interpretation, therefore, that such defendants served quasi-prison sentences. Additionally, the researcher acknowledges that the courts, as an institution, do not provide defendants with compensation for their time in remand when they are not guilty. Consequently, the researcher interpreted the institutional practice of remand as causing a negative externality for defendants. This led the researcher to interpret such practices as embodying the value of procedural adversity.

Fourth and finally, a small number of defendants announced that they wanted to give a false and early guilty plea because the process was too long. Such occurrences were sparse. Still, the researcher believed that the issue (defendants being motivated to give false guilty pleas) was significant enough to warrant reporting. The two following example extracts demonstrate such defendant motivations. For context, Extract 5.9 shows a brief conversation between a legal advisor and a magistrate before the court hearing began. Here, the defendant appeared from live link. Meanwhile, Extract 5.10 shows the remarks of a defendant who the court found not guilty of driving-related offences.

Extract 5.9

Defendant:	Well. What would happen to me if I pleaded now?
Legal advisor:	What? Erm, sorry?
Defendant:	So, if I pleaded guilty now, could I get tried here?
Legal advisor:	… Erm, why would you want to plead guilty, Mr Defendant?
Defendant:	Well, it doesn't change anything does it? … if I just plead now, I can get it out the way, I would rather just get it done now.
Legal advisor:	The allegation is 'intent to supply'.

Defendant: Yes, and I never wanted to do that.
Legal advisor: No, no, well the magistrates won't allow that obviously.

Extract 5.10

Defendant: If I would have knew that the court would have been as long as this, I would have just taken the fine and paid the £100!

In both extracts, the defendants explain that being found wrongfully guilty was preferential to attempting to establish their innocence through the summary justice process. In Extract 5.9, this appears to be the case because of the adversity associated with a prolonged process. This is particularly evident where the defendant states, "if I just plead now, I can get it out the way, I would rather just get it done now". Meanwhile, in Extract 5.10, the defendant, who was eventually found not guilty by the court, explained that the proposed fine of £100 would have been less punishing than undergoing the court process. These two example extracts draw attention to how a lengthy summary justice process can reportedly be more punishing than a formal, judicial sentence. For this reason, the researcher arrived upon the interpretation that the observed justice embodied the value of procedural adversity.

5.4 Summary

This chapter has demonstrated how court users' procedural adversity was a defining theme (or overarching value) of the observed summary justice process. In support of this claim, this chapter has shown how victims would experience emotional difficulties during the oral evidence-in-chief process because of how they had to narrate their own victimization. Relatedly, this chapter has drawn upon observational data to show how solicitors' use of cross-examination often entwined emotionally intense accusations of disbelief, making the process emotionally difficult for victims and witnesses. Similarly, this chapter has presented observational data showing how the cross-examination process compelled court users to explain issues of an intimate/sensitive nature, further rendering the process an emotionally difficult one. Furthermore, the data has demonstrated how the justice process was inconvenient for defendants because they were required to travel significant distances to attend court hearings (justice was non-local). Additionally, some defendants reportedly experienced adversity because they had to forgo paid work in order to attend court hearings. Another difficult part of the justice process for defendants was the experience of remand, where they were still technically innocent but were required to remain in custody. Lastly, a small number of defendants announced that they wanted to give a false and early guilty plea because they found the length of the summary justice process too punishing. Section 6.4 delves deeper into these findings, critically analysing how such challenges for court users should be viewed as a form of inefficiency that undermines the overall quality of the justice process. Indeed, rather than these findings being used to argue that the justice process is overly efficient, Section 6.4 uses the present chapter's data analysis to argue that the summary justice process is not efficient enough.

SIX

Overcoming Over-Efficiency

6.1 Introduction

Building from the prior data analysis chapters, this chapter makes the argument that the courts are largely characterized by the concept of over-efficiency, as described in Section 1.3. Sections 6.2 and 6.3 support this argument by critically discussing the data analysis of Chapters 3 and 4. These sections explain how the observed courts eroded the quality of justice by prioritizing speediness and standardization to the detriment of substantiating values, which include verdict accuracy, sentence proportionality, defendant comprehension and institutional legitimacy among others. Indeed, the observed courthouse's prioritization of efficiency, in speed and standardization-based terms, rendered the summary justice process overly efficient. Following this, Section 6.4 develops from the initial data analysis of Chapter 5, drawing attention to how there is room for the summary justice process to become more efficient from a court-user-focused perspective. In making this argument, this final chapter demonstrates to readers the need to frame efficiency dynamically, as initially described in Chapter 1: to recognize that efficiency can be for quality justice, but it must play a secondary role to other substantiating values.

The final portion of this work offers readers some grounded-in-practice, evidence-based policy reform ideas for improving the summary justice process. The focus here is predominantly on mitigating the problem of over-efficiency. To this end, this final chapter utilizes the conceptual framework of Section 1.3 to identify ways that the summary justice process can improve.

6.2 Slower justice is better justice (in the right places!)

To begin, the present work takes issue with district judges' mid-hearing plea-bargaining practices, as described in Section 3.2 (see Extract 3.5). When district judges encouraged defendants to give a guilty plea in exchange for an immediate and favourable sentence, this deprioritized the value of fairness. Indeed, in the researcher's view, this practice of district judges worked against Article 6.2 of the Human Rights Act 1998, which ensures the right to a fair trial. Under this article, the court should operate with the presumption that defendants are innocent until proven guilty (through the trial process). Given that the district judge in Extract 3.5 engaged in a plea bargain mid-hearing, that is, before a full trial had taken place, suggests that the judge operated from the presumption that the defendant was guilty. In this way, the process deprioritized fairness (from a human rights perspective) in favour of speed-focused managerialism. And as human rights align with substantiated justice (as explained in Section 1.3), the present work concludes that the observed mid-hearing plea-bargaining practices of district judges diminished the substantiveness of the summary justice process.

Additionally, district judges' speedy mid-hearing plea bargaining deprioritized the value of verdict accuracy. This practice deprioritized the value of verdict accuracy because it was unclear why defendants pleaded guilty following a district judge's plea bargain. A similar issue is described by Covey (2009: 73) and Dervan (2012) and is known as the 'innocence problem' (first discussed in Section 2.4). Indeed, when plea bargains are used to motivate a guilty plea from a defendant before a trial has taken place, it becomes unclear why a defendant pleads guilty. It may be because they were factually guilty and the plea bargain was able to successfully elicit this truth. Alternatively, the motivation to plead guilty may emanate from a drive to omit a prolonged, risky, punishing process despite being factually innocent (originally described in Feeley, 1992). It is unknown which of these two narratives are true of the observed practices in Section 3.2. As successful plea bargains omit the fact-finding portion of the summary justice process (the trial), plea bargains also omit a verdict based on an adversarial test of evidence, degrading the accuracy of verdicts produced by the justice process. In this way, while the plea-bargaining practices of district judges may have had an efficiency (speedy justice) benefit, overall they diminished the quality of the justice process because they deprioritized a value that primarily substantiates the justice process (verdict accuracy). Rephrased, such practices were not for quality justice, they were for over-efficiency.

Critics of this assessment may argue that the observed plea-bargaining practices of district judges were for quality justice, as they combined both speediness and victim-focused justice. This is a view that has been similarly held regarding the use of the early guilty plea scheme (first discussed in Section 2.4). The Ministry of Justice (2012: 28) has reflected such a perspective when commenting on how 'swift justice' is desirable not just for its intrinsic speediness benefits but also because it is victim focused. Indeed, 'justice delayed is justice denied' (Herbert in Ministry of Justice, 2012: 3; see Section 1.3). On a surface level analysis, there is some evidence to support this claim. As unpacked in Section 3.2, the plea-bargaining practices of district judges resulted in speedy case disposals. Additionally, and as emphasized by the district judge in Extract 3.5, such speedy case disposals could save victims and witnesses the inconvenience of attending court, effectively resulting in victim-focused justice.

Despite this, the present study maintains that this form of efficiency does not go far enough to preserve the substantiveness of the summary justice process, even from a victim-focused perspective. This critical view of plea-bargaining practices similarly reflects the concern of Bibas (2003: p 172); namely, 'judges should focus less on efficiency and more on moral education, reform, catharsis, and healing'. Indeed, if an offender does plead guilty, but only begrudgingly (without remorse) in order to secure a discounted or lesser sentence, is this victim-focused justice? Bibas (2003) argued that it is not, as none of the meaningful reform work that makes justice a victim-satisfactory process has taken place. The present work agrees with this assessment. Furthermore, as explained in Section 1.3, procedural due process (which encompasses the robust protection of human rights) is central to substantiating the summary justice process. To this end, while the observed plea-bargaining practices produced some benefits (speediness and possibly a weak form of victim-focused justice), they were not enough to preserve the substantiveness of the process (procedural due process as defined by court practices robustly prioritizing human rights and verdict accuracy). As a result, this work does not accept the interpretation that the observed mid-hearing plea-bargaining practices of district judges were for quality justice.

Second, magistrates' voluntary absence from the courtroom, as exemplified in Extract 3.6, contributed to the problem of over-efficiency. As outlined in Section 3.2, magistrates often stepped out of the courtroom, allowing other professional staff to resolve case management issues among themselves. While this hands-off leadership style led to quicker case resolutions, it also meant magistrates reduced their role in providing democratic oversight to the justice process. This is problematic because the role of a magistrate and the justice they deliver in the lower criminal courts is grounded in their democratic contributions (previously discussed in Sections 1.3 and 2.4; see Sanders, 2001). Therefore, magistrates could improve the quality of the observed justice process by remaining in court and providing more extensive democratic oversight during such case management discussions. Indeed, this change may well lead to slower but better justice.

Third, solicitors' in-court, pre-hearing/trial planning practices that prioritized speediness also problematically deprioritized thorough fact-checking. As explained throughout Section 3.3 with various example extracts, solicitors would often work cooperatively to manage case files just before hearings took place. Here, solicitors would jointly decide the reliability of witness testimony, what the criminal charges should be, as well as whether a defendant was guilty. This gave the observed solicitors' performances a pseudo-adversarial/theatrical character during formal hearings (similarly described in Ball, 1975). Indeed, in the researcher's interpretation, such practices omitted sincere and zealous adversarial fact-checking between the prosecution and defence during formal case management hearings. Rephrased, justice outcomes were not reflective of thorough fact-checking, rather they embodied a cooperative spirit that prioritized immediate case progression/finality through compromise. This prioritization of cooperative efficiency (speediness) which is to the detriment of thorough fact-checking is a form of over-efficiency.

Fourth, and similarly to the previous point, prosecution solicitors' non-contesting of mitigating factors deprioritized the value of thorough fact-checking that is traditionally upheld in adversarial practices. As Section 3.3 has explained, prosecution solicitors would rarely challenge the evidence which supported mitigating factors. This practice would mean that the process, while speedy, would not investigate evidential points that could affect the proportionality of criminal sentences. As exemplified by Extract 3.11 in Section 3.3, such uncontested mitigating factors made it unclear whether the defendant had stopped using alcohol/drugs, taken on new carer duties and was genuinely motivated to engage with criminal justice services. Indeed, in this example extract, the prosecution did not investigate the factualness of these factors. If sentencers accepted such factors as truthful, as they did in Extract 3.11, when they were factually not true, then inaccurate sentence outcomes would follow, diminishing the quality of justice. Rephrased, the courts uncontested acceptance of mitigating factors resulted in them accepting a dubious view of the 'burdens and benefits of social life' regarding the offender, negatively affecting the proportionality of criminal sentences (Heffernan, 2000: 49; previously discussed in Section 1.3). The speediness described in Section 3.3, therefore, was for over-efficiency, not for efficiency in a quality justice sense.

A concern of the researcher is that solicitors' deprioritization of adversarial-based fact-checking in favour of speediness may reflect a deeper problematic issue: a novel form of game-playing. To briefly reiterate Section 2.4, the Criminal Procedure Rules (CPRs) were, in part, designed to discourage adversarial game-playing in the form of 'fishing expeditions' and 'warehouse disclosures' (Department for Constitutional Affairs, 2006: 25; also see Auld, 2001). Applied to the aforementioned practice of solicitors' cooperativeness over adversarialism, it is the researcher's concern that solicitors may be working together for their shared self-interests rather than primarily for the interests of justice. Namely, and reflecting a concern raised in Nicklas-Carter's (2019) work, rapid case disposals may be primarily serving defence solicitors by increasing the number of legal aid/private cases they can accept/dispose of, which subsequently increases their revenue (previously discussed in Section 2.4). Meanwhile, Crown Prosecution Service solicitors may primarily seek rapid case disposals simply for relief from their increasingly concentrated workloads. Together, defence and prosecution solicitors may be prioritizing speediness because it primarily serves their interests rather than what would work primarily in favour of a substantiated, thoroughly investigated judicial outcome. While this game-playing dimension of the process is speculative, it would nonetheless negatively affect the substantiveness of the summary justice process. It could be a root cause of the aforementioned form of over-efficiency.

Additionally, district judges' proactive leadership practices may be encouraging this speculative form of game-playing. As unpacked in Section 3.2, district judges operated as court workgroup leaders, pressuring both defence and prosecution solicitors to prioritize speedy case disposals above that of other values (see Extracts 3.1–3.4). To this end, the proactive leadership of district judges may have an enabling character, giving tacit permission for both the defence and prosecution to engage in game-playing so long as it results in speedy justice.

Fifth, legal advisors' muting of defendants during live link hearings deprioritized the value of defendant participation and, relatedly, procedural fairness. To briefly reiterate from Section 3.4, it was common for defendants to be muted for large portions of their live link hearing to allow court staff to speedily dispose of cases without interruption or distraction. As a consequence, however, defendants seemingly could not fully contribute/participate vocally to the process. This observation connects with the view of Tyler (2003; also see Section 1.3), who has argued that procedural fairness is at least partly connected to how defendants view the court as engaging with them and listening to their concerns. Given that legal advisors would purposely limit a defendant's voice to the minimum required for speedy case disposal purposes, the researcher takes the view that defendants were not adequately engaged in the process. Rephrased, the observed summary justice process prioritized speediness over defendant participation. This practice negatively affected the substantiveness of the process in favour of speediness, resulting in the problem of over-efficiency.

This analysis links with the work of Gibbs (2017) and McKay (2018) who have commented on how live link hearings have a tendency to marginalize and dehumanize defendants (first discussed in Section 2.4). As Gibbs (2017) has argued, muting practices can dehumanize defendants; it can render the justice process as something that is being done to them rather than something that they are involved in. McKay's (2018) Australian work has drawn attention to the potential severity of these muting practices: some defendants may be muted at both ends, unable to speak and hear for large portions of proceedings. This is concerning because it is plausible that this severe type of control is occurring in the observed English and Welsh summary justice processes. Indeed, the courts integration of live link technology may well have played an enabling role for a severe form of over-efficiency.

Sixth, the court workgroup's quick processing of cases deprioritized the value of procedural fairness and defendant comprehension. To briefly reiterate Section 3.4, the court workgroup would secure speedy case disposals through cooperatively managing defendants' participation (their voice and comprehension) in the courtroom, not just when using live link. These controlling practices did indeed promote speedy case disposals (see the data analysis of Extracts 3.14–3.19). Problematically, however, these practices also reflect the concerns raised by Tyler (2007). Namely, Tyler (2007) emphasized that procedural fairness is connected to how defendants feel listened to by judicial staff (see Section 1.3). As defendants could not raise their concerns before the court and therefore be listened to and contribute in a way that they viewed as valuable, the speedy justice processes of Section 3.4 deprioritized the value of procedural fairness. Additionally, as discussed in Section 1.3, comprehensibility is a key value that substantiates the justice process (see European Commission for the Efficiency of Justice, 2016). Therefore, given that the process prioritized speediness at the expense of defendant comprehension, the researcher is of the view that the observed practices were, again, not supportive of quality justice. Indeed, such practices warrant the attention of reformers, to help reduce the problem of over-efficiency in the criminal court process.

This analysis connects and builds from Welsh's (2016: 151; 2022) argument that 'high degrees of co-operation tend to marginalize defendants from active participation in the proceedings' (see Section 2.4). As similarly argued in the present work, the court workgroups' cooperative managerialism resulted in speedy justice while also marginalizing defendants. A central contention drawn to in Welsh's (2016) research was that defendants are not a homogenous group, they often have 'different issues and defendants are likely to have different priorities' (Welsh, 2016: 173). To this end, and as argued by Feeley (1992), a slow process can be the primary punishment for court users and these defendants may therefore approve of their marginalization in the process granted that the process becomes faster (previously discussed in Section 2.4). Meanwhile, other defendants may indicate that they would prefer a slower process with their greater involvement in it, so as to work against what some may experience as a dehumanizing process (as argued in Welsh, 2016; Gibbs, 2017). The usefulness of the present research is that it provides additional evidence to demonstrate that defendants actively sought clarity from court staff when they did not understand proceedings, emphasizing their desire to comprehend the summary justice process. Indeed, as demonstrated in Section 3.4, defendants would make their concerns known to the court and, sometimes, they would offer suggestions regarding how they could gain greater comprehension of the process, such as through the use of a post-hearing receipt (see Extracts 3.17, 3.18 and 3.19). Section 6.5 develops from this point further, unpacking how this study offers implications for future research and considerations for policy reformers.

Lastly, the court workgroup's reliance on offenders as a means information source deprioritized the value of sentence proportionality and, connectedly, institutional legitimacy. As established in Section 3.4, the court workgroup would rely on defendants to provide speedy but likely inaccurate means information about themselves in court. While somewhat self-evident, rapid but inaccurate means information negatively impacted sentencers' capacity to formulate proportionate sentences (which includes fines, compensation orders and victim surcharge costs). This tolerance for inaccurate means information negatively affected the legitimacy of the courts. Indeed, criminal sentences were not impartial: criminals effectively played a role in deciding how severely they should be punished and court sentences not only tolerated but motivated this practice (again, see Extract 3.21). Rephrased, the present analysis argues that the process was overly efficient because of how it prioritized rapid case disposals (speediness) over procedural due process values (sentence proportionality and institutional legitimacy).

6.3 Less standardization, more specialization

The findings of Section 4.2 align with the broader literature that recommends limiting pro-streamlining managerial reforms in the criminal justice process. Indeed, to briefly reiterate Section 4.2, the researcher observed court staff processing defendants who were evidently living with mental health issues in the same way as non-mental health affected defendants. Additionally, the researcher observed court staff occasionally wanting to divert a defendant from the criminal justice process but being unsure how to action such a procedure. In both of these situations, the summary justice process was not characterized by the value of defendant safeguarding, which could have taken the form of well-executed specialist court practices such as diversion. Rather, the process was for standardization. This observation is similar to that described in Welsh's (2016: 67; 2022) work, where she has highlighted how the court workgroup is committed to 'routinization', which often has a marginalizing affect on court users (previously discussed in Section 2.4). Additionally, the observations of Section 4.2 resonate with the Australian lower criminal court work of Mack and Roach Anleu (2007: 341; also see Section 4.2), who have argued that court staff are primarily focused on 'getting through the list', reflecting a commitment to streamlined managerialism.

Indeed, as unpacked in Section 4.2, the court workgroup seemed[1] to be more centrally concerned with processing cases systematically in a routine, standardized manner rather than addressing court users' apparent mental health difficulties (that is, actively engaging in defendant safeguarding). Consequently, in the researcher's interpretation, the observed practices were for over-efficiency: court practices were committed to the managerial value of standardization to the detriment of adequately safeguarding vulnerable defendants.

Second, magistrates' and judges' presumed disbelief regarding the claimed mental health issues of defendants deprioritized the value of fair sentencing. As unpacked in Section 4.2, sentencers would openly announce their scepticism of defendants' mental health claims, both when the defendant was and was not present. It is possible that the reported mental health issues of defendants were factually true and so severe that they (should have) significantly impacted sentencing, or possibly exculpated them. Indeed, Article 6(2) of the Human Rights Act 1998 compels the court to presume a defendants' innocence until proven otherwise. Therefore, when court staff operated from a position of disbelief regarding the potentially exonerating claims of mental health-affected defendants, they effectively denied them the right to be presumed innocent.

At the same time, the present work recognizes that the criminal justice process is for quality when it appropriately adjusts for social disadvantage which includes poor mental health (see 'social justice' in Section 1.3). Again, given that court staff operated from a position of disbelief regarding defendants claimed mental health issues, the process was not supportive of this form of social disadvantage. Reframed, this lack of adjustment for mental health affected defendants negatively and impacted fair sentencing in a social justice sense. While these practices are compatible with a traditional conception of managerial efficiency because of how it favours standardization, they were not for quality justice in the researcher's interpretation.

Third, sentencers' standardized approach to sentencing substance-related offenders, which relied on moral reprimands and comments on responsibilization, deprioritized the value of rehabilitative sentencing. Indeed, sentencers always viewed offenders' substance use as an aggravating factor (see Extract 4.6), rather than a victimizing and/or mitigating factor. This was despite offenders seemingly candid remorse regarding their substance-related behaviour (see Extract 4.7), and despite these offenders seemingly candid desire for support in order to overcome their addictions (see Extract 4.8). It is unclear to what extent (if at all) the criminal actions of defendants with such conditions should be deemed culpable and worthy of punishment. However, it must be presumed that, at least sometimes, an offender has sincerely attempted to overcome a substance addiction, failed despite their best efforts and then while under the influence of a substance, committed an offence they wholeheartedly regretted. Under these circumstances, such uniform moral reprimands and responsibilization comments would self-evidently not be for quality justice.[2] This is an observation which connects with Bibas's (2003) work, which has argued against the standard, traditional retributive criminal justice approach and instead has argued for a greater focus on rehabilitation or 'healing' specifically regarding substance abuse cases (similarly discussed in Liebenberg et al, 2013; Donoghue, 2014a; Snedker 2018a, 2018b). This refocus on healing rather than punishment (which entails the aforementioned moral reprimands and responsibilization components) is more aligned with social justice ideas. Indeed, a rehabilitative sentencing process that adjusts for a defendant's unique difficulties in overcoming substance use/addiction is more for quality justice than one which is effectively blind to it, that uniformly morally reprimands and responsiblizes all offenders.

Fourth, and related to the prior point, the courts' focus on punitive sentencing for defendants with multiple and severe forms of disadvantage deprioritized the value of social justice-oriented problem-solving. To briefly reiterate Section 5.4, defendants would often live with multiple forms of disadvantage and commit crimes that were related to sustenance and/or personal protection concerns. See, for example, the analysis of Extract 4.20 which centres on how a homeless individual required food, so resorted to theft. Alternatively, see Extract 4.21, which focuses on how a defendant owned a bladed article because they (allegedly) feared for their safety while being street homeless. Despite magistrates/district judges recognizing such social injustice, they would sentence such offenders similarly to that of non-disadvantaged offenders in a standardized and somewhat factory-like, punitive manner. This observation provides further support to the literature's assessment that criminality is often entwined with complex and connected forms of social disadvantage which requires specialized processes to resolve (see Duncan and Corner, 2012; Donoghue, 2014a, 2014b; Bramley et al, 2015; see Section 3.2). In this way, the present work joins the proverbial chorus of voices that draws attention to the historic problem of a standardized lower criminal court process: it is inadequate for addressing multiple and severe (compounded) disadvantage cases. Indeed, the observed summary justice process missed an opportunity to promote greater social justice, that is, to address social disadvantage that influences criminal behaviour. To this end, the observed justice could have been of greater quality.

As a caveat to the prior two points, the researcher observed some drug rehabilitation requirement (DRR) hearings that embodied a limited form of social justice-oriented, problem-solving. As previously discussed in Section 4.3, DRR hearings embodied a more relaxed character, as magistrates explored defendants' significant life events and challenges. In doing so, these court practices stepped away from being myopically focused on the individual and their alleged moral and responsibility failures and examined wider, holistic issues that contribute to offending (such as poor housing, employment, relationships, and so on). However, and as commented upon in Section 4.3, the degree to which these hearings upheld the value of therapeutic-based problem-solving is questionable. Indeed, the observed magistrates, being lay people, were ill-equipped to navigate complex social issues in other people's lives (such as addiction and bereavement; see Extracts 4.14 and 4.16). While the direction of these hearings was for quality justice in that they attempted to uphold rehabilitative/therapeutic, problem-solving values, this could have been done in a more acute fashion – possibly in a purely professional setting out of court. At the same time, such DRR hearings were incredibly rare, operating in only one courtroom, one day per week.[3] Consequently, it is the view of the present researcher that the magistrates' courts could improve quality of justice by more strongly moving towards specialization, which may well require relying more on external professional services.

Fifth, and in addressing the caveat point from Section 4.4, defence solicitors' drive to secure lengthy sentences for their clients deprioritized the value of institutional legitimacy. To briefly reiterate the initial analysis of Extract 4.23, defence solicitors would paradoxically argue for their client to receive lengthy prison sentences because, they maintained, it would help to alleviate the social disadvantage of their client. Indeed, defence solicitors candidly explained that they believed that prison was a place where social disadvantage (such as homelessness and drug addiction) could be effectively resolved. Evidentially, the standardized summary justice process is ill-equipped to address social disadvantage without inevitably punishing/relying on prison, or, at least, so the observed solicitors argued. This brings into question the capacity of the courts to deliver justice. Indeed, to use Packer's (1968: 56) phraseology, a criminal sentence that conflates punishment with rehabilitation is a form of 'gratuitous cruelty'; it is not for justice in a basic theoretical sense. These practices, therefore, diminished the legitimacy of the observed lower criminal court process.

This prior critical discussion point connects with the other observations of Section 4.4, regarding how court staff would regularly vocalize their dissatisfaction with how the lower criminal courts processed disadvantaged defendants/offenders. Indeed, staff would complain about institutional constraints and the limitations of the process to address defendants multiple and compounded forms of social disadvantage which connects to offending behaviour (see Extract 4.22). These comments, alongside the aforementioned pro-prison stance of defence solicitors, suggest that the summary justice process cannot meaningfully facilitate social justice in its present configuration. This limitation is a point of inefficiency. The courts have a capacity to become more efficient by developing processes that resolve social disadvantage (promoting greater social justice) while simultaneously resolving factors that entwine with criminality/reoffending (effectively reducing the courts' future workload).

6.4 Efficiency as an adversity-free process

In the prior two sections, this work has argued that the observed summary justice process of Chapters 3 and 4 was largely characterized by the problem of over-efficiency. The present section moves beyond this argument, drawing attention to how the observed summary process as described in Chapter 5 was inefficient from a court-user-focused perspective. The central argument of this section, therefore, is that the courts should become more efficient in terms of making the process less of a burden for court users. This section also draws attention to how a more efficient justice process (a adversity-free process) can free itself up to more robustly uphold justice-substantiating values. In this way, this section argues that the summary justice process has a capacity to not only become more efficient but to be more for substantiated justice as well.

To begin, the observed practices of Section 5.3 promoted verdict inaccuracy, undermining the quality of justice. Indeed, the researcher observed how defendants who experienced remand and/or a lengthy justice process were motivated to give an early and false guilty plea (see Extracts 5.9 and 5.10). These observed problematic practices advance the work of Feeley (1992: 199), demonstrating how, for many defendants, it continues to be the case that the process is the 'primary punishment'. Furthermore, the present work lends support to Marsh's (2016) assessment that government-sponsored reports (such as Leveson, 2015a) have overlooked those processes that generate inaccurate verdicts. This study, therefore, adds to the existing literature by encouraging policy makers to address the problem of procedural adversity in the summary justice process, and the subsequent verdict inaccuracy that follows from it.

Second, oral evidence-in-chief and cross-examination practices deprioritized the value of court-user safeguarding. To briefly reiterate Section 5.2, the researcher observed that the investigatory, oral evidence-giving portions of the summary justice process had a negative emotional impact on court users (see the analysis of Extracts 5.1, 5.2, 5.3 and 5.4). This critical discussion point connects with the issues raised in Adler's (1987) work regarding how the justice process has a capacity to re-victimize because of the emotionally demanding, oral evidence-giving phase of the process (also see Lees, 2002; Smith, 2018). The present work advances the literature by demonstrating how such re-victimization takes place in the lower criminal courts, rather than just with victims/survivors of rape in Crown Court trials. As perhaps a more novel contribution to the socio-legal literature, the present work draws attention to the capacity of the summary justice process to negatively impact defendants who are themselves vulnerable during the oral evidence-giving process (see the analysis of Extract 5.4). Indeed, the process can victimize defendants by eroding their dignity, that is, by having them narrate events that are emotionally difficult for them. While the researcher acknowledges that evidence testing is a key aspect of the justice process, emotional distress is not a necessary component. Consequently, this work argues that the observed summary justice process has a capacity to become more for substantiated justice, while reforms that preserve fact-finding and reduce adversity may require creative thinking.

Third, case listing practices deprioritized the value of accessible justice, thereby undermining the quality of justice. As established in Section 5.3, defendants would often travel long distances to attend a court hearing, resulting in non-local justice which likely also incurred some financial costs (see Extract 5.5). Additionally, defendants reported that they would often forgo paid work in order to attend court, further inconveniencing them (see Extract 5.6). Travel expenses and missed paid work likely produced a significant barrier for court users in terms of their capacity to attend court, beyond the issue of pragmatic inconvenience (which again, the present work recognizes as a form of inefficiency from a court users' perspective). Lower criminal court users are typically from lower socioeconomic backgrounds (also see Ward, 2016); this may well, therefore, produce a dilemma for court users: either choosing economic security or participation in the justice process (regardless of whether the court compels their attendance). To this end, the researcher interpreted current institutional case listing practices as deprioritizing the value of accessible justice. As discussed in Section 1.3, accessibility is a value that works towards substantiating the justice process. Therefore, the researcher takes the view that the current summary justice process warrants reform. Namely, the summary justice process could be for greater quality (accessibility) by reforming case listing practices that are presently characterized by procedural adversity.

Lastly, remand practices deprioritized the value of procedural fairness. To briefly reiterate the data analysis of Section 5.3, the researcher collected evidence demonstrating that defendants found their experiences of remand emotionally distressing. In the researcher's view, these practices worked against the value of procedural fairness because the process required defendants (who the court had not yet found guilty of a crime) to experience quasi-prison sentences. Indeed, time spent in remand resembled a punishment as the court forcibly withheld the liberty of unconvicted people, in a manner that would have been typical of a prison sentence (similarly argued in Cheng, 2013a, 2013b; Baughman, 2017; previously discussed in Section 2.4).

As a consequence of this, the use of remand during the observation period embodied a Schrödinger[4] character: defendants' occupancy in remand was both a punishment and not a punishment at the same time; the court would only discover which outcome it definitively was once the defendant's guilt was decided. This paradox regarding the allegedly just forced detention of unconvicted people is reflected in the Home Affairs Committee's 2004 report. Indeed, this report encouraged policy makers to frame remanded, presumed-innocent defendants as 'unconvicted prisoners' (s.252). In this system, if a defendant is found guilty, their time in remand is used to off-set their criminal sentence. Simultaneously, if a remanded defendant was found to be not guilty, their time in the cells was not recognized as a punishment (and, therefore, these individuals could not pursue compensation for wrongful imprisonment). To this end, the Home Affairs Committee would appear to embrace the idea that remand makes use of 'Schrödinger cells', which function as both a punishment and not at the same time, only firmly switching into one of the positions once a sentencer decides a defendant's guilt. This is indeed, procedurally unfair.

While the researcher acknowledges that remand serves a public protection role, public protection does not have to necessitate procedural adversity (pre-emptive punishment practices) (similarly argued in Baughman, 2017). Consequently, the present work recognizes such remand practices as an area of focus for policy reformers: such practices should be reformed to better promote the values of public protection and procedural fairness.

6.5 Reforms recommendations

First, the CPRs should make explicit that district judges should not engage in plea bargaining mid-hearing/during trials. As discussed in Section 2.4, a principal role of the CPRs is to govern the cooperative, in-court practices of court staff in view of efficiency concerns (see Auld, 2001; Department for Constitutional Affairs, 2006; Leveson, 2015a). While these rules presently focus on the behaviour of defence and prosecution parties, there appears to be no reason why the rules should not be expanded to govern the role of judges. Indeed, as first described in Section 3.2, judges did engage in speed-focused cooperative behaviour with the defence party, namely, plea bargaining. And as argued in Section 6.2, such practices deprioritized the value of verdict accuracy, undermining the quality of the justice process. Therefore, in order to ensure the proper governance of the criminal court process (to protect it from becoming overly efficient), policy makers should revise the CPRs to prohibit such mid-hearing/trial plea-bargaining practices.

Second, the summary justice process should provide defendants with an immediate in-court receipt of proceedings. More specifically, the court (a legal advisor and/or usher) should provide defendants with an in-court, post-hearing written summary that details: the hearing's outcome (such as bail conditions or sentencing impositions), key dates/times of upcoming hearings, key tasks that court staff are to complete between hearings (such as the disclosure of evidence or the compiling of a probation report) as well as who is going to attend future hearings and why. This reform recommendation follows from the critical discussion of Section 6.2, regarding how the court workgroup prioritized speediness over ensuring defendants' comprehension of the court process, eroding quality of justice. Indeed, by defendants having a greater knowledge of when and how they can contribute to the justice process, they could avoid time-consuming and frustration-inducing confrontations with court staff (as observed in Extracts 3.14, 3.15 and 3.16 in Section 3.4). In doing so, the process could more robustly uphold the values of defendant comprehension and participation alongside the value of speediness. Rephrased, by providing defendants with immediate post-hearing receipts, the summary process could become more efficient in a quality justice sense.[5]

Third, the defence should make use of evidence at the collaborative level when presenting mitigating factors during sentencing hearings. The critical discussion of Section 6.2 supports this reform recommendation, specifically regarding how the prosecution would often not contest the factualness of mitigating factors, which resulted in speedy but likely disproportionate sentences (over-efficiency). This recommendation would mean that the defence party could not present mitigating factors based on a defendant's testimony alone, as the researcher observed in Section 3.3. Rather, the court should raise the standard of proof required to present mitigating factors to the collaborative level. Meaning, the court should only accept mitigating factor claims that are supported by two forms of evidence (such as oral testimony with supporting document-based evidence). A benefit of this reform is that it may discourage the defence from raising erroneous mitigation claims, which presently the defence can evidence on their client's oral testimony alone (a problem demonstrated in Extract 3.11; see Section 3.3). The present study envisions that this new duty on the defence could speed up the process by encouraging the defence party to omit presenting erroneous mitigation claims, thereby reducing the workload of the courts. At the same time, the process could produce more proportionate sentences, as sentencers are able to draw upon more substantial evidence that details the severity of mitigating factors.

Critics may argue that a problem with the aforementioned reform is that a defendant who has a genuine mitigation claim but is unable to provide collaborative evidence will not receive proportionate justice. In view of this problem, reformers should remember that truth claims, or the burden of truth, relies on the claiming party. Therefore, if the defence argues that a defendant is characterized by mitigating factors, they must present evidence of a reasonable level that supports this claim – the defendant's oral testimony alone cannot be framed as trustworthy/reasonable evidence. To do otherwise would be to undermine the truth-finding mission of the courts, which is a key principle that substantiates the justice process (as first discussed in Section 1.3). Furthermore, this concern can be minimized with the allocation of proper legal aid services that work to ensure the facts of a case are brought to court, which would entail helping defendants acquire such collaborative evidence. In conclusion to this point, therefore, this reform could challenge current court practices that are for over-efficiency by promoting greater sentence proportionality while simultaneously omitting unnecessary (erroneous) mitigation processes.

Fourth, His Majesty's Courts and Tribunals Service (HMCTS) should provide court staff with refresher training regarding their role in the diversion process. The critical discussion of Section 6.3 supports this reform recommendation, specifically regarding how court staff were unfamiliar with how to action the diversion process and how court staff appeared to overlook signs that defendants were living with severe mental health conditions/needs (first discussed in Section 4.2). Indeed, by court staff receiving additional mental health diversion process training, they may be better able to connect appropriate disadvantage-addressing services (liaison and diversion) to those individuals who require them (defendants with mental health conditions), consequently improving quality of justice. This reform recommendation also draws attention to the Bradley Report (Department of Health, 2009) and its claim that liaison and diversion (L&D) services can produce efficiency in terms of reducing courthouse caseloads by appropriately diverting cases out of the courts while simultaneously promoting more appropriate resolutions for vulnerable court users (see Section 2.4). The present reform recommendation serves to promote this same end.

Fifth, the CPRs should make explicit that the defence party cannot advocate for a defendant to receive a lengthier prison sentence than what the prosecution is advocating for. This reform recommendation follows from the critical discussion of Section 6.3, regarding how defence solicitors viewed prison as a rehabilitative place that could resolve defendants' social disadvantage such as that regarding substance addiction and homelessness. The present work takes the view that defence solicitors should instead request that their client receive a rehabilitation activity requirement (as is otherwise typical of defence advocacy). Alternatively, defence solicitors should request that the court divert their client from the criminal justice process entirely or that their client should make use of specialized court processes depending on the severity and type of their client's disadvantage. This reform recommendation may well form part of a wider structural change in the criminal justice process (for example, by allowing the summary justice process to have greater involvement in the allocation of social housing, as one magistrate suggested in Section 4.4 – see Extract 4.22). Rephrased, the present work takes the view that the summary justice process can better safeguard vulnerable defendants with multiple and severe forms of social disadvantage by prohibiting pro-prison defence advocacy, thereby improving quality of justice in the lower criminal courts.

Lastly, the court should prompt defendants regarding reimbursements for travel expenses at the end of the in-court process. As Section 5.3 has established, justice is often non-local, demanding that defendants travel significant distances to attend court. At the same time, the researcher acknowledges that the court estates closure programme has been expanding (see Section 2.4), further reducing how the courts uphold the value of accessible and local justice (see Section 6.4). To this end, the researcher takes the view that the courts' utilization of greater travel compensation for defendants is a reasonable mitigating step to bolster access to justice and, therefore, promote justice quality. More specifically, the present research proposes the modest reform that the court workgroup should prompt defendants about travel compensation at the end of each in-court proceeding.[6] In this way, the summary justice process would operate to mitigate travel costs that obstruct accessible justice, and thus promote quality of justice.

6.6 Future research directions

First, the literature would benefit from further research regarding court staff and their potential speed-focused game-playing (described in Section 6.2). As discussed in Section 6.2, a concern of the present research is that solicitors may be engaging in a novel form of cooperative, speedy justice game-playing that works towards advancing their own interests rather than the interests of justice (somewhat similarly discussed in Auld, 2001; see Section 2.4). As also suggested in Section 6.2, district judges may be enabling this speedy justice game-playing. These practices warrant further research to better understand how future summary justice policy reforms, such as modifications to the CPRs (see Section 2.4) should promote cooperativeness. Indeed, legislators' recent push for greater cooperativeness among court staff may well have had an inadvertent, detrimental effect on the quality of summary justice that is not fully understood by reform thinkers. Therefore, in the interest of preserving quality justice in the courts, researchers should further explore this cooperative gaming issue.

Second, further research is required to help define what specific, additional provisions are required for magistrates to better engage with disadvantaged defendants. As argued in Section 6.3, magistrates would make use of problematic responsibilization comments and morally reprimanded socially disadvantaged offenders, undermining the quality of the justice process. There were also institutional barriers that limited magistrates' ability to support social justice; for example, see Extract 4.22 where a magistrate wanted to provide social housing to a defendant but could not. While the present work recognizes that other thinkers such as Ward (2016: 129) have found evidence to support the claims that magistrates can act as 'social justice innovators', the present work depicts a more multifaceted, complex account of magistrates in the summary justice process. Indeed, magistrates appeared to want to support social justice ends but often did not know how to do this. Alternatively, magistrates seem to believe that reprimanding individuals for being socially disadvantaged had some beneficial effect, as poorly founded as this may seem to others (also discussed in Section 6.3). This leads the present work to conclude that the role of magistrates has the potential to become more for social justice, but additional provisions are required to enable them to better engage with disadvantaged defendants. However, how this should happen in practical, reform recommendation-based terms is unclear. Indeed, magistrates may require additional training in some capacity (for example, to better understand how addiction is not a moral failing) or there should be a greater joining up of services (such as social housing services with the courts) to empower magistrates to more robustly uphold social justice-related values. Further research on this issue could help specify more concretely how to render magistrates more firmly as social justice innovators/champions.

Relatedly, further research is required to better understand what sort of social disadvantage cases magistrates should not engage with, so as to promote a process that can better uphold social justice values. While the 'social justice innovator' contributions of magistrates can be positive (as discussed by Ward, 2016: 129), future policy reform should also recognize that magistrates are not rehabilitation/therapeutic professionals (as emphasized in Section 6.3). Magistrates should be limited, therefore, to those cases that do not require professional levels of knowledge to provide appropriate, non-problematic advice to disadvantaged individuals.

At the same time, the present work recognizes Miller's (in Donoghue, 2014a: xx) concern that the introduction of therapeutic/rehabilitative professionals can result in the 'courtification' of key social services (as first discussed in Section 2.4). Indeed, by effectively replacing magistrates with social service professionals/external services, this could render the lower criminal courts as gate keepers of key services and, at the same time, this could have an undesirable criminal justice net-widening effect (also discussed by Miller in Donoghue, 2014a). The present research, therefore, affirms that there is some theoretical space between the work of Donoghue (2014a), Ward (2016) and that of Miller (in Donoghue, 2014a) that warrants the attention of summary justice researchers. Magistrates' social justice innovator role is desirable but they cannot (and should not) act as rehabilitative/therapeutic professionals, which current problem-solving courts (DRR hearings) allow. It is unclear how such complex social disadvantage cases should be resolved within the summary justice process without introducing gate keeper and net-widening problems. For this reason, this is an area that warrants further research.

Third, legal advisors' muting practices warrant further research to explore their extent and impact. As Section 6.2 has discussed, the researcher was unsure whether defendants were able to fully hear/view proceedings during live link hearings. Indeed, it was unclear to what extent court staff controlled communication channels during live link courtroom proceedings, owing to the present study's observation-only method. It is possible that criminal justice staff muted all communication channels for defendants, rendering them unaware of what was being said in their hearings. Staff may have done this because it is advantageous from a speedy justice perspective: it could ensure that a defendant would not interject/protest, which would have slowed down proceedings. In view of this, the present study supports further research in this area, to allow policy makers to better understand the full impact of live link technology on the court process and how this affects quality of justice, with specific attention given to the powerful/controlling role of legal advisors. At the same time, in view of the capacity of live link to deprioritize the value of defendant participation, the present study places pressure on policy reformers to limit any further expansion of live link/video conferencing technologies, echoing the sentiments of Gibbs (2017). Indeed, expansion should be halted until there is a deeper understanding of the impact of conferencing tools, and, if necessary, until appropriate protective measures are well established.

Fourth, further research would be useful to better understand how the courts can more reliably collect and utilize means information for proportionate sentencing purposes. As established in Section 6.2, the courts would use offenders as a source of means information in order to secure speedy case disposals. This, however, deprioritized the courts' commitment to proportionate sentencing. In view of this over-efficiency problem, this work recommends that the courts utilize third-party services to more reliably obtain an offender's financial means. For example, it may be possible for legal advisors to use digital records from His Majesty's Courts and Tribunals Service in conjunction with data sets from the Department of Work and Pensions to speedily supply sentencers with up-to-date, accurate means information. This would promote greater efficiency (rather than over-efficiency) as the process could prioritize proportionate sentencing while also supporting speedy case outcomes. Additionally, this reform could more robustly preserve the image of the courts as a fair, legitimate institution because of its renewed focus on impartiality. How such a reform could be actioned in a concrete, technical sense is beyond the scope of the present work because of a lack of IT expertise and access to government services. It is notable, however, that this recommendation is in step with the Ministry of Justice's (2012) and government advocates' drive for joined-up services/efficiency through technology (similarly argued in Department for Constitutional Affairs, 2006; Leveson, 2015a; see Chapter 2). To this end, it is rational for the government to lead such specialist future research.

Fifth, there should be further research into how the courts can mitigate against the slowing down of the justice process which is caused by defendants' self-representation (DIY) practices. As detailed in Section 3.4, when a defendant represented themselves at court (engaged in a DIY defence), they bottlenecked the flow of the court process. This analysis reflects the concerns of Marris (in HC Deb 1 January 2017: col 119wh) as well as Doward and Dare (2016) regarding how the Legal Aid, Sentencing and Punishment of Offenders Act 2012 (LASPO) may promote defendant self-representation which then causes the process to become 'clogged up' (first discussed in Section 2.4). However, due to its design, the present research cannot establish a direct correlation between LASPO and an increase in self-representation, as it lacks observational data prior to LASPO's introduction. The usefulness of the present observational study is to simply spotlight how such self-representation practices do indeed take place in the contemporary summary justice process; and importantly, these practices were not for quality justice in either social justice, procedural due process or efficiency terms. To this end, the only reasonable recommendation the present work can make is to emphasize that further research may be able to shed light on how to improve such DIY defence practices. This may well mean reinstating pre-LAPSO levels of legal representation.

Sixth, another area warranting further research is to identify methods to reduce the distressing elements of the oral evidence-giving process that impacts defendants, complainants/victims and witnesses in the summary justice process. As detailed in Section 6.4, lower criminal court users have reported distress due to the oral evidence process. This observation aligns with findings from Crown Court researchers which have focused on victims/survivors of rape (see Adler, 1987; Lees, 2002; Smith, 2018). The contribution of the present study is to sensitize researchers to how current practices in the lower courts should be enhanced to protect all court users, thereby elevating the overall quality of the justice process. Due to its broad scope, this study could not provide robust, evidence-based recommendations for reform. Consequently, the present work encourages further specialist research here: to examine how the lower criminal courts can operate in a way that better promotes court-user safeguarding during the oral evidence-giving process.

Lastly, further research should investigate how to mitigate against the summary justice process motivating early and false guilty pleas. As Section 6.4 has critically discussed, the courts use of remand coupled with a lengthy justice process placed pressures on defendants to give false and early guilty pleas, undermining quality of justice. At the same time, this study recognizes that this is a complicated area for policy reform because of how remand upholds the value of public safety, another quality justice-assuring value. Consequently, while the present research firmly demonstrates that current remand practices are problematic, what is to be done about this in concrete policy reform terms is unclear. Again, this is owing to the limited, exploratory nature of the present study. Therefore, the present work identifies this issue as a subject for future specialist research.

6.7 What does the future of the criminal courts look like?

This work has offered readers a unique insight into the lower criminal court process of England and Wales, arguing that there are practices which are for 'over-efficiency'. Indeed, as evidenced in this study, there are practices which prioritize efficiency (speediness and standardization) above values that substantiate justice, which primarily relate to procedural due process and social justice. These include but are not limited to verdict accuracy, sentence proportionality, defendant comprehension and accessible justice. These practices therefore warrant reform in order to bolster the quality of the justice process.

This study's over-efficiency criticism of the summary justice process may come as a surprise to some readers. Over the last few decades, numerous government reports have consistently argued that the criminal justice process needs to become more efficient, typically in speed and technology-enabled terms. While these efficiency reform thinkers have no doubt been benevolent in their intentions, this work's observational data depicts the lower criminal courts as a justice factory more than it does a place where delicate social problems are carefully considered and resolved. Policy makers' prior conceptualizations of efficiency in the criminal justice process have evidently been poor.

At the same time, it is important to make clear that efficiency is not inherently undesirable, nor should be absolutely avoided by policy reformers. To the contrary, this study has demonstrated how more efficiency in the right places and with the right priorities can contribute to improving the quality of the justice process. Indeed, as argued in this chapter, the process should become more efficient in terms of being less adversity-laden for court users. This form of efficiency is supportive of quality justice because it does not erode procedural due process or social justice-related values. Future policy makers would benefit from incorporating this approach into their own reform design framework: efficiency is desirable, but it should always play a secondary role to the more important concerns of social justice and procedural due process.

So, what will the future of the criminal courts look like? A better justice system is possible. This work has argued for that by offering a range of evidence-based policy reforms that aim to fix (at least partially) the problem of over-efficiency in the summary justice process. At the same time, this study has identified areas for further research with the hope that future social scientists, criminologists and socio-legal researchers will explore and re-evaluate the role of efficiency in the criminal courts. The goal of this work has been to improve the justice system for those who experience it and for our society that benefits from it. The success of this book should be measured by the degree to which it achieves this end.

Notes

one Introduction

1 In greater detail, MacDonald (2008: 28) argues that Packer (1968) sometimes uses the term efficiency in the sense that the police are reliable finders of truth ('investigative efficiency'). Meanwhile, in other extracts, MacDonald (2008: 28) demonstrates that Packer (1968) uses the term efficiency to mean that the courts operate speedily when assigning verdicts of guilt and innocence ('operational efficiency'). Finally, MacDonald (2008: 25) also argues that Packer (1968) sometimes uses the term efficiency to mean that a reliable criminal process can have a deterrent effect ('deterrent efficacy').

2 This is a point similarly held by Berlin (2002: 217) when discussing 'the pluralism of values'. Namely, 'the very desire for guarantees that our values are eternal and secure in some objective heaven is perhaps only a craving for the certainties of childhood or the absolute values of our primitive past' (Berlin, 2002: 217).

3 For example, see MacDonald's (2008: 28) 'investigative efficiency'. This is an ideal-type because it relies on the police/prosecution being inerrant, infallible truth seekers. This is, of course, an impossible reality. As Weber explains, an ideal-type of this kind is a 'mental construct [that] cannot be found empirically anywhere in reality' (in MacDonald, 2008: 46). Such theoretical constructions are useful because they aid thinkers in analysis and exposition. However, they cannot be used for practical policy reform recommendations because of their extreme characteristics.

4 Heffernan's (2000: 80) influential essay makes a similar observation to MacDonald (2008) when it comments upon 'normative pluralism'. Namely, Heffernan (2000) believes that social justice can mean different things when applied to the criminal justice process because of its interpretative basis: 'there are multiple, inconsistent, conceptions of social justice. Each of these conceptions is relevant to the different components of criminal justice – to formulations of the rules of criminal procedure and also to formulations of excuses and justifications. Thus, each generates different, and often irreconcilable, policy conclusions for criminal justice.' Rephrased more whimsically, social justice is like apple pie: while virtually everyone is in favour of it, there are 'many different varieties of apple!' (Powell et al, 2011: 1).

5 Similarly, the European Commission for the Efficiency of Justice (2016; ECEJ hereafter) has focused on how human rights should be upheld in

the justice process in order to secure justice quality. The ECEJ (2016: 13) has argued that there are a range of values or 'pillars of quality' that substantiate the justice process, these include publicity and transparency (open justice), adequate legal assistance and comprehensibility.

two The Modern History of Summary Justice Efficiency

1 This drive towards individualism has also been framed as the 'responsibilisation' of the citizenry, especially when referring to the recipients of state services (see Liebenberg et al, 2013: 1).

2 See MacDonald (2008: 2) regarding the 'strong-ideal-type'.

3 Legal aid is an English and Welsh public service that was established with the Legal Aid and Advice Act 1949. The purpose of legal aid is to allow English and Welsh court users to have 'access to justice', that is, to provide court users with legal advice and representation if they cannot afford it themselves (Hynes and Robins, 2009; Mant, 2017).

4 There are four notable government-sponsored reports: (1) Auld's (2001) *Review of the Criminal Courts of England and Wales*, (2) Falconer's *Delivering Simple Speedy, Summary Justice* (Department of Constitutional Affairs, 2006), (3) the Ministry of Justice's (2012) White Paper, *Swift and Sure Justice* and, finally, (4) Leveson's (2015a) *Review of Efficiency in Criminal Proceedings*.

5 Albeit, Adisa (2018: 7) reported mixed results regarding the reduction of physical courthouses. While economic benefits for the court were notable, Adisa (2018: 40) argued that 'as things stand, it would be difficult to say that access to justice has not been compromised, diminishing the quality of justice of the courts. It is worth noting, however, that Adisa's 2018 study was of the Suffolk area only. Therefore, these results may not be generalizable to all courts across England and Wales.

6 This seems to reflect the view of Crown Prosecution Service staff regarding live link: 'A disappointingly low proportion of CPS staff (17.9%) thought that the introduction of digitisation [live link] had been effective in improving the quality of service to victims and witnesses' (Her Majesty's Crown Prosecution Service Inspectorate and Her Majesty's Inspectorate of Constabulary, 2016: 42).

7 See the Court Estate Reform Programme 2010, and the 2015 and 2018 programmes of the same name (Ministry of Justice, 2018).

8 Winick and Wexler (2003) explain that therapeutic jurisprudence (TJ) does not have a single agreed upon definition. Yet, the literature largely agrees that it is for rehabilitative ideals which are health and wellbeing promoting. This can take the form of criminal processes and sentences that are for 'healing' offenders who have substance abuse/addiction issues (Schma, 2003:87).

9 To explain further, in England and Wales, if criminal justice practitioners suspect that a defendant is living with a mental health disorder, they are to inform liaison and diversion (L&D) staff who are then obligated to screen the suspected defendant (as directed under the NHS England Liaison and Diversion Programme, 2014; also see Mental Health Act 1983 revised 2007, s.39; Department of Health, 2009; Reed, 1992). Following this screening, if L&D staff confirm that the defendant is living with a mental health disorder, these staff can then divert the defendant from the standardized criminal court process ensuring that such vulnerable people receive more appropriate services/treatment. To this end, court staff have a responsibility to refer/initiate diversion proceedings if they suspect that a defendant is living with a mental health disorder (NHS England Liaison and Diversion Programme, 2014).

10 While the government has continued to experiment with problem-solving courts since the closure of the NLCJC, these have only been through the use of small pilot programmes (further discussed in Donoghue, 2014a; Home Office, 2023).

11 Miller (in Donoghue, 2014a: xx) gives somewhat tacit support for this view, as they argue that a criticism of problem-solving justice is its capacity to produce the 'courtification' of social welfare. In greater detail, Miller's concern is that the criminal courts may become a necessary and unreliable step for seeking social/medical aid (in Donoghue, 2014a). For Miller, this type of process is undesirable because it risks serving in a gate-keeping capacity for wider social services (in Donoghue, 2014b).

12 Indeed, it is for this reason that Donoghue (2014a: 101) frames the government's closure of the NLCJC as, 'very unfortunate: it was an innovation that was supported by many exceptionally dedicated professionals who were determined to bring a more "community focused" and "therapeutic" approach to the court system when compared to traditional case processing'.

three Speed-Focused Managerialism

1 The court usher made this comment directly to the researcher during the observation period. Indeed, it was not uncommon for court staff to make remarks to the researcher, owing to the researcher's regular appearance at the courthouse.

2 'DIY defence' practices are described in Section 2.4.

3 In this hearing, the defendant was expected to present evidence in support of the argument that they would undergo exceptional hardship if their driving licence was revoked. This was a penalty that was imposed against them from a prior hearing. Such exceptional hardship cases typically focus on how the defendant has family or work commitments that centre on

driving and, therefore, the court should make an exception in their case and not revoke their driving licence despite the number of points they have accumulated.

four Standardized Defendant Processes

1 Defendants were addicted to a range of substances. No single substance was prominent throughout the collected data. Addictions to alcohol, synthetic cannabinoids ('spice'), cocaine, heroin and methamphetamine were all commonly reported.

2 During the data collection period, the researcher observed specialist (non-standard) drug rehabilitation requirement hearings (sometimes referred to as drug courts or DRR courts by staff) (also discussed in National Offender Management Service, 2014). These were significantly different to the vast majority of the other observed hearings in terms of the courtroom's physical layout, the social tone of proceedings (involving all of those present) and the pacing of the proceedings. Section 2.4 discusses these specialized courts further.

3 The Ministry of Justice and HM Prison and Probation Service (2023: 66) provides technical detail regarding what a 'RAR' is.

six Overcoming Over-Efficiency

1 Emphasis is given to the word 'seemed' here. A limitation of the present study is its observation-only design (as further discussed in Section 6.6). Indeed, the researcher was unable to examine the supporting court records for each hearing (such as whether liaison and diversion services were consulted).

2 Sentencers would sometimes make use of probation orders (including rehabilitation activity requirements) that were rehabilitative. However, their moral reprimands and responsibilization comments remained the same. Indeed, and to reiterate, this was a standardized component of the observed sentencing process which evidently, would not always be appropriate.

3 In total, the observed courthouse made use of thirteen courtrooms allocated to adult-related hearings. In this context, DRR hearings were indeed a rare occurrence.

4 See the now widely cited Schrödinger's cat paradox (1935). A comparison is made here between the unknowability of phenomenon until it is observed and the unknowability of whether defendants' custody time is a punishment until a sentencer announces a verdict of guilt.

5 It is also noteworthy that this post-hearing receipt recommendation is supported with the comments of defendants (see Extracts 3.18 and 3.19 in Section 3.4).

6 It is worth emphasizing that this reform would be well situated within existing legislation, see The Costs in Criminal Cases (General) Regulations 1986 (s.23), which facilitates for the courts to order costs to defendants for travel expenses (also see Berke, 2021).

References

Adisa, O. (2018) *Access to Justice: Assessing the Impact of the Magistrates' Court Closures in Suffolk*. Suffolk: Suffolk Institute for Social and Economic Research.

Adler, Z. (1987) *Rape on Trial*. London: Routledge.

Ashworth, A. (1979) Concepts of Criminal Justice. *Criminal Law Review*, 26: 412–27.

Ashworth, A. and Redmayne, M. (2010) *The Criminal Process*. Oxford: Oxford University Press.

Auld, R. (2001) *Review of the Criminal Courts of England and Wales*. London: The Stationery Office.

Ball, M. (1975) The Play's the Thing: An Unscientific Reflection on Courts under the Rubric of Theater. *Stanford Law Review*, 28(1): 81–115.

Banerjee, J. and Smith, R. (2018) *Civil and Criminal Solicitors' Views on LASPO*. London: BVA BDRC.

Barendrecht, M., Kistemaker, L., Scholten, H., Schrader, R. and Wrzesinska, M. (2014) *Legal Aid in Europe: Nine Different Ways to Guarantee Access to Justice?* Netherlands: WODC.

Barry, B. (2005) *Why Social Justice Matters*. Cambridge: Polity Press.

Baughman, S. (2017) Costs of Pretrial Detention. *Boston University Law Review*, 97(1): 1–30.

BBC (2004) *Full Text: Blair on Law and Order*. [online] BBC.com. Available from: http://news.bbc.co.uk/1/hi/uk_politics/3907651.stm [Accessed 1 December 2020].

Bell, E. (2011) *Criminal Justice and Neoliberalism*. London: Palgrave Macmillan.

Berke, D. (2021) *How to Claim Court Expenses and Legal Costs if You Are Acquitted*. [online] Factuk.org. Available from: https://factuk.org/how-to-claim-court-expenses-and-legal-costs-if-you-are-aquitted/ [Accessed 1 December 2021].

Berlin, I. (2002) *Liberty*. Oxford: Oxford University Press.

Bhattacharjee, A. (2018) Right to Legal Aid: An Integral Part of Social Justice. *International Journal of Research and Analytical Reviews*, 5(3): 999–1001.

Bibas, S. (2003) Using Plea Procedures to Combat Denial and Minimization. In B. Winick, and D. Wexler (eds) *Judging in a Therapeutic Key: Therapeutic Jurisprudence and the Courts, Vol. II.* Durham, NC: Carolina Academic Press.

Bohm, R. (2006) 'McJustice': On the McDonaldization of Criminal Justice. *Justice Quarterly*, 23(1): 127–46.

Bowcott, O. (2014) *Judges Criticise Impact of Legal Aid Cuts.* [online] *The Guardian.* Available from: https://www.theguardian.com/law/2014/may/14/judges-legal-aid-cuts [Accessed 4 January 2020].

Boyle, K., Hadden, T. and Hillyard, P. (1980) *Ten Years on in Northern Ireland. The Legal Control of Political Violence.* London: Civil Liberties Trust.

Bramley, G., Fitzpatrick, S., Edwards, J., Ford, D., Johnsen, S., Sosenko, F. and Watkins, D. (2015) *Hard Edges Mapping Severe and Multiple Disadvantage.* London: Lankelly Chase Foundation.

Brodie, S. (2011) *The Cost to Justice Government Policy and the Magistrates' Courts.* London: POLITEIA.

Burnett, I. (2018) *The Lord Chief Justice's Report 2018.* London: Judicial Office.

Cheng, K. (2013a) Pressures to Plead Guilty: Factors Affecting Plea Decisions in Hong Kong Magistrates' Courts. *British Journal of Criminology*, 53(2): 257–75.

Cheng, K. (2013b) The Guilty Plea Process in the Hong Kong Magistrates' Courts Early Guilty Plea, PhD thesis, The University of Hong Kong.

Contempt of Court Act (1981) [online] Available from: http://www.legislation.gov.uk/ukpga/1981/49 [Accessed 5 January 2020].

Cook, D. (2006) *Criminal and Social Justice.* London: Sage Publishing.

Costs in Criminal Cases (General) Regulations 1986, The. [online] Available from: https://www.legislation.gov.uk/uksi/1986/1335/contents/made [Accessed 7 January 2020].

Covey, R. (2009) Signalling and Plea Bargaining's Innocence Problem. *Washington & Lee Review*, 66: 73–130.

Cowie, G. and Sturge, G. (2019) *Court Closures and Access to Justice.* [online] parliament.uk. Available from: https://commonslibrary.parliament.uk/research-briefings/cdp-2019-0156/ [Accessed 3 March 2024].

Criminal Justice Act (2003) [online] Available from: http://www.legislation.gov.uk/ukpga/2003/44/contents [Accessed 4 January 2020].

Criminal Procedure Rules 2020. [online] Available from: https://www.legislation.gov.uk/uksi/2020/759/contents/made [Accessed 14 October 2023].

Crown Prosecution Service (2015) *Transforming Summary Justice: A Criminal Justice System-Wide Initiative to Improve How Cases are Dealt with in the Magistrates' Courts.* [online] www.cps.gov.uk. Available from: https://www.cps.gov.uk/publication/transforming-summary-justice-criminal-justice-system-wide-initiative-improve-how-cases [Accessed 7 July 2019].

Crown Prosecution Service (2020) *Coronavirus: Interim CPS Case Review Guidance – Application of the Public Interest Covid-19 Crisis Response.* [online] www.cps.gov.uk. Available from: https://www.cps.gov.uk/legal-guidance/coronavirus-interim-cps-case-review-guidance-application-public-interest-covid-19 [Accessed 14 October 2023].

Davies, M. (2005) A New Training Initiative for the Lay Magistracy in England and Wales – A Further Step towards Professionalisation. *International Journal of the Legal Profession*, 12(1): 93–119.

Deering, J. and Feilzer, M. (2015) *Privatising Probation: Is Transforming Rehabilitation the End of the Probation Ideal.* Bristol: Policy Press.

Department for Constitutional Affairs (2006) *Delivering Simple, Speedy, Summary Justice.* London: Department for Constitutional Affairs.

Department of Health (2009) *The Bradley Report: Lord Bradley's Review of People with Mental Health Problems or Learning Disabilities in the Criminal Justice System.* London: Department of Health.

Dervan, L. (2012) Bargained Justice: Plea-Bargaining's Innocence Problem and the Brady Safety-Valve. *Utah Law Review*, 1: 51–98.

Dillow, C. (2007) *The End of Politics: New Labour and the Folly of Managerialism*. Petersfield: Harriman House.

Donoghue, J. (2014a) *Transforming Criminal Justice: Problem-Solving and Court Specialisation*. London: Routledge.

Donoghue, J. (2014b) Reforming the Role of Magistrates: Implications for Summary Justice in England and Wales. *The Modern Law Review*, 77(6): 928–63.

Donoghue, J. (2017) The Rise of Digital Justice: Courtroom Technology, Public Participation and Access to Justice. *The Modern Law Review*, 80(6): 995–1025.

Doward, J. and Dare, T. (2016) *Legal Aid Cuts Have Led to Surge in DIY Defence, Says Charity*. [online] *The Guardian*. Available from: https://www.theguardian.com/law/2016/apr/23/legal-aid-cuts-defendants-unrepresented [Accessed 4 January 2020].

Duff, P. (1998) Crime Control, Due Process and 'The Case for the Prosecution': A Problem of Terminology? *British Journal of Criminology*, 38(4): 611–15.

Duncan, M. and Corner, J. (2012) *Severe and Multiple Disadvantage: A Review of Key Texts*. London: Lankelly Chase Foundation.

European Commission for the Efficiency of Justice (2016) *Measuring the Quality of Justice*. Europe: Council of Europe.

Feeley, M. (1992) [1979] *The Process Is the Punishment: Handling Cases in a Lower Criminal Court*. New York: Russell Sage Foundation.

Feeley, M. and Simon, J. (1992) The New Penology: Notes on the Emerging Strategy of Corrections and Its Implications. *Criminology*, 30(4): 449–74.

Fitzpatrick, P., Seago, C. and Wall, D. (2000) New Courts Management and the Professionalisation of Summary Justice in England and Wales. *Criminal Law Forum*, 11: 1–22.

Galligan, D. (1996) *Due Process and Fair Procedures: A Study of Administrative Procedures*. Oxford: Clarendon Press.

Gibbs, P. (2017) *Defendants on Video – Conveyor Belt Justice or a Revolution in Access?* London: Transform Justice.

Harcourt, B. (2010) Neoliberal Penality: A Brief Genealogy. *Theoretical Criminology*, 14(1): 74–92.

Harvey, D. (2005) *A Brief History of Neoliberalism*. Oxford: Oxford University Press.

HC Deb (1 January 2017) vol 619, col 119wh. Available from: https://hansard.parliament.uk/Commons/2017-01-11/debates/0C8BB50A-A1F3-448C-B853-E674FAA39426/AccessToJustice [Accessed: 4 January 2020].

Heffernan, W. (2000) Social Justice/Criminal Justice. In W. Heffernan and K. Kleinig (eds) *From Social Justice to Criminal Justice: Poverty and the Administration of Criminal Law*. Oxford: Oxford University Press.

Her Majesty's Courts and Tribunals Service (2016) Modernisation of Justice through Technology and Innovation. [online] www.gov.uk. Available from: https://www.gov.uk/government/speeches/modernisation-of-justice-through-technology-and-innovation [Accessed 4 January 2020].

Her Majesty's Crown Prosecution Service Inspectorate and Her Majesty's Inspectorate of Constabulary (2016) Delivering Justice in a Digital Age: A Joint Inspection of Digital Case Preparation and Presentation in the Criminal Justice System. London: HMCPSI, HMIC.

Home Affairs Committee (2004) *Home Affairs – First Report*. [online] publications.parliament.uk. Available from: https://publications.parliament.uk/pa/cm200405/cmselect/cmhaff/193/19302.htm [Accessed 14 October 2023].

Home Office (2023) *Problem Solving Courts Pilots in the Police, Crime, Sentencing and Courts Bill: Equalities Impact Assessment*. [online] Gov.uk. Available from: https://www.gov.uk/government/publications/police-crime-sentencing-and-courts-bill-2021-equality-statements/problem-solving-courts-pilots-in-the-police-crime-sentencing-courts-bill-equalities-impact-assessment [Accessed 8 January 2020].

Hood, C. (1991) A Public Management for All Seasons? *Public Administration*, 69(1): 3–19.

Hood, C. and Scott, C. (1996) Bureaucratic Regulations and New Public Management in the United Kingdom: Mirror-Image Developments? *Journal of Law and Society*, 23(3): 321–45.

Horne, J. (2016) A Plea of Convenience an Examination of the Guilty Plea in England & Wales, PhD thesis, University of Warwick.

House of Commons Committee of Public Accounts (2023) *Progress on the Courts and Tribunals Reform Programme: Sixty-First Report of Session 2022–23*. [online] Available from: https://committees.parliament.uk/publications/40649/documents/198166/default/ [Accessed 3 March 2024].

House of Commons Justice Committee (2015) *Impact of Changes to Civil Legal Aid under Part 1 of the Legal Aid, Sentencing and Punishment of Offenders Act 2012*. London: The Stationery Office.

House of Commons Justice Committee (2016) *The Role of the Magistracy*. London: Parliament.uk.

House of Commons Justice Committee (2019) *Court and Tribunal Reforms, Second Report of Session 2019*. London: The Stationery Office.

Human Rights Act (1998) [online] Available from: http://www.legislation.gov.uk/ukpga/1998/42/contents [Accessed 3 January 2020].

Hynes, S. and Robins, D. (2009) *The Justice Gap: Whatever Happened to Legal Aid?* London: Legal Action Group.

Johnston, E. and Smith, T. (2017) The Early Guilty Plea Scheme and the Rising Wave of Managerialism. *Criminal Law & Justice Weekly*, 181: 210–12.

Jones, C. (1993) Auditing Criminal Justice. *British Journal of Criminology*, 33(2): 187–202.

Judiciary of England and Wales (2018) *The Lord Chief Justice's Report 2018*. London: Judicial Office.

Laster, K. (1990) Legal Interpreters: Conduits to Social Justice? *Journal of Intercultural Studies*, 11(2): 15–32.

Law Society (2017) *Access Denied? LASPO Four Years on: A Law Society Review*. London: The Law Society of England and Wales.

Le Vay, J. (1989) *Magistrates' Courts Report of a Scrutiny, Volume 1*. London: Her Majesty's Stationery Office.

Lees, S. (2002) *Carnal Knowledge: Rape on Trial* (2nd edn). London: The Women's Press.

Legal Aid Agency (2018) *Interests of Justice Guidance on the Consideration of Defence Representation Order Applications*. London: Legal Aid Agency.

Legal Aid, Sentencing and Punishment of Offenders Act (2012) [online] Legislation.gov.uk. Available from: http://www.legislation.gov.uk/ukpga/2012/10/contents/enacted [Accessed 4 January 2020].

Leveson, B. (2015a) *Review of Efficiency in Criminal Proceedings*. London: Judiciary of England and Wales.

Leveson, B. (2015b) Increasing Efficiency in Criminal Justice whilst Respecting Human Rights. In Judiciary of England and Wales, JUSTICE Annual Human Rights Conference, UK, 12 October 2015. England: JUSTICE.

Liebenberg, L., Ungar, M. and Ikeda, J. (2013) Neo-Liberalism and Responsibilisation in the Discourse of Social Service Workers. *British Journal of Social Work*, 10: 1–16.

Ludlow, A. (2015) *Privatising Public Prisons: Labour Law and the Public Procurement Process*. London: Hart Publishing.

Macdonald, S. (2008) Constructing a Framework for Criminal Justice Research: Learning from Packer's Mistakes. *New Criminal Law Review*, 11(2): 257–311.

Mack, K. and Roach Anleu, S. (2007) 'Getting Through the List': Judgecraft and Legitimacy in the Lower Courts. *Social & Legal Studies*, 16(3): 341–61.

Magistrates Association (2022) *It Shouldn't Cost to Volunteer.* [online] Magistrates-association.org.uk Available from: https://www.magistrates-association.org.uk/publication/it-shouldnt-cost-to-volunteer/ [Accessed 3 March 2024].

Mant, J. (2017) Neoliberalism, Family Law and the Cost of Access to Justice. *Journal of Social Welfare and Family Law*, 39(2): 246–58.

Marsh, L. (2016) Leveson's Narrow Pursuit of Justice: Efficiency and Outcomes in the Criminal Process. *Common Law World Review*, 45(1): 51–67.

McBarnet, D. (1978) False Dichotomies in Criminal Justice Research. In J. Baldwin and A. Bottomley (eds) *Criminal Justice Selected Readings*. London: Martin Robertson.

McBarnet, D. (1981) *Conviction: Law the State and the Construction of Justice*. London: Palgrave Macmillan.

McConville, M. and Marsh, L. (2015) Adversarialism Goes West: Case Management in Criminal Courts. *The International Journal of Evidence & Proof*, 19(3): 172–89.

McKay, C. (2018) *The Pixelated Prisoner*. New York and London: Routledge.

Menkel-Meadow, C. (2019) Uses and Abuses of Socio-Legal Studies. In N. Creutzfeldt, M. Mason and K. McConnachie (eds) *Routledge Handbook of Socio-Legal Theory and Methods*. Abingdon: Routledge.

Mental Health Act (1983) [online] Available from: http://www.legislation.gov.uk/ukpga/1983/20/contents [Accessed 06 March 2024].

Merton, R. (1952) *Reader in Bureaucracy*. New York: Macmillan.

Ministry of Justice (2005) *The Objectives and Content of the First Criminal Procedure Rules*. Justice.gov.uk. [online] Available from: https://www.justice.gov.uk/courts/procedure-rules/criminal/notes [Accessed 5 January 2020].

Ministry of Justice (2012) *Swift and Sure Justice: The Government's Plans for Reform of the Criminal Justice System*. London: The Stationery Office.

Ministry of Justice (2013) *Transforming the CJS: A Strategy and Action Plan to Reform the Criminal Justice System*. [online] Gov.uk. Available from: https://assets.publishing.service.gov.uk/government/uploads/system/uploads/attachment_data/file/209659/transforming-cjs-2013.pdf [Accessed 3 March 2024].

Ministry of Justice (2016a) *Response to the Proposal on the Provision of Court and Tribunal Services in the Midlands Region*. [online] Gov.uk. Available from: https://consult.justice.gov.uk/digital-communications/proposal-on-the-provision-of-court-and-tribunal-es/results/mids-consultation-response.pdf [Accessed 3 March 2024].

Ministry of Justice (2016b) *Transforming our Justice System: Summary of Reforms and Consultation*. [online] Gov.uk. Available from: https://consult.justice.gov.uk/digital-communications/transforming-our-courts-and-tribunals/supporting_documents/consultationpaper.pdf [Accessed 3 March 2024].

Ministry of Justice (2018) *Fit for the Future: Transforming the Court and Tribunal Estate*. [online] Gov.uk. Available from: https://consult.justice.gov.uk/digital-communications/transforming-court-tribunal-estate/supporting_documents/hmctsstrategyapproachconsultation.pdf [Accessed 3 March 2024].

Ministry of Justice (2020) *The Objectives and Content of the First Criminal Procedure Rules – Criminal Procedure Rules*. [online] Justice.gov.uk. Available from: https://www.justice.gov.uk/courts/procedure-rules/criminal/notes-tables/notes [Accessed 1 December 2021].

Ministry of Justice & HM Prison & Probation Service (2023) *Sentence Management in the Community Policy Framework*. [online] assets.publishing.service.gov.uk. Available from: https://www.gov.uk/government/publications/sentence-management-in-the-community-policy-framework#:~:text=This%20policy%20framework%20provides%20a,of%20their%20sentence%20in%20the [Accessed 14 October 2023].

Morgan, R. (2012) Crime and Justice in the 'Big Society'. *Criminology & Criminal Justice,* 12(5): 463–81.

Morgan, R. and Russell, N. (2000) *The Judiciary in the Magistrates' Courts*. London: Home Office.

National Audit Office (2014) *Implementing Reforms to Civil Legal Aid*. London: National Audit Office.

National Audit Office (2016) *Efficiency in the Criminal Justice System*. London: NAO Communications.

National Audit Office (2023) *Progress on the Courts and Tribunals Reform Programme*. London: NAO Communications Team.

National Offender Management Service (2014) *Supporting Community Order Treatment Requirements*. [online] Gov.uk. Available from: https://assets.publishing.service.gov.uk/government/uploads/system/uploads/attachment_data/file/426676/Supporting_CO_Treatment_Reqs.pdf [Accessed 8 January 2020].

NHS England Liaison and Diversion Programme (2014) *Liaison and Diversion Operating Model 2013/14*. London: NHS England.

Nicklas-Carter, C. (2019) Efficiency of the English Criminal Courts in a Time of Austerity. Exploring Courtroom Lawyers' Assessment of Government Policy (2010–2017), PhD thesis, Keele University.

O'Malley, P. (2010) Fines, Risks and Damages: Money Sanctions and Justice in Control Societies. *Current Issues in Criminal Justice*, 21(3): 365–81.

Packer, H. (1968) *The Limits of the Criminal Sanction*. Stanford, CA: Stanford University Press.

Powell, M., Johns, N. and Green, A. (2011) *Social Justice in Social Policy*. Social Policy Annual Conference, Lincoln. [online] Available from: https://social-policy.org.uk/previous-conferences/2011-conference/ [Accessed 1 January 2023].

Prosecution of Offenders Act (1995) [online] Available from: https://www.legislation.gov.uk/ukpga/1985/23#:~:text=F1An%20Act%20to%20provide,and%20section%203%20of%20the [Accessed 3 January 2024].

Raine, J. (1993) Perspectives on Quality in the Magistrates' Court Service. *Justice of the Peace*, February: 85–8.

Raine, J. (2001) Modernising Courts or Courting Modernisation? *International Journal of Public Sector Management*, 13(5): 390–416.

Raine, J. and Willson, M. (1993) *Managing Criminal Justice*. Harlow: Harvester Wheatsheaf.

Raine, J. and Willson, M. (1995) New Public Management and Criminal Justice. *Public Money & Management*, 15(1): 35–40.

Raine, J. and Willson, M. (1997) Beyond Managerialism in Criminal Justice. *The Howard Journal of Criminal Justice*, 36(1): 80–95.

Reed, J. (1992) *Mentally Disordered Offenders – Review of Health and Social Services for Mentally Disordered Offenders*. London: Priority and Health Services Division.

Rhodes, R. (1996) The New Governance: Governing without Government. *Political Studies*, 44: 652–67.

Ritzer, G. (1993) *The McDonaldization of Society*. Thousand Oaks, CA: Pine Forge Press.

Rossetti, P. (2015) *Waiting for Justice: How Victims of Crime Are Waiting Longer than Ever for Criminal Trials*. London: Victim Support.

Rutherford, A. (1993) *Criminal Justice and the Pursuit of Decency*. Sheffield: Waterside Press.

Sanders, A. (2001) *Community Justice: Modernising the Magistracy in England and Wales*. London: Institute for Public Policy Research.

Sanders, A. (2002) Core Values, the Magistracy, and the Auld Report. *Journal of Law and Society*, 29(2): 324–41.

Sanders, A., Young, R. and Burton, M. (2010) *Criminal Justice* (4th edn). Oxford: Oxford University Press.

Schma, W.G. (2003) Judging for the New Millenium. In B. Winick and D. Wexler (eds) *Therapeutic Jurisprudence and the Courts, Vol. I*. Durham, NC: Carolina Academic Press.

Schrödinger, E. (1935) Die gegenwärtige Situation in der Quantenmechanik (The present situation in quantum mechanics). *Naturwissenschaften*, 23(48): 807–12.

Sentencing Council (2004) *Overarching Principles: Seriousness*. London: Sentencing Guidelines Secretariat.

Sentencing Council (2016) *Reduction in Sentence for a Guilty Plea Guideline Consultation*. London: Sentencing Council.

Sentencing Council (2017) *Reduction in Sentence for a Guilty Plea – First Hearing on or after 1 June 2017*. [online] Sentencingcouncil.org.uk. Available from: https://www.sentencingcouncil.org.uk/overarching-guides/magistrates-court/item/reduction-in-sentence-for-a-guilty-plea-first-hearing-on-or-after-1-june-2017/ [Accessed 4 January 2020].

Smith, B. (2004) The Role and Influence of District Judges the Magistrates' Courts, PhD thesis, University of Leicester.

Smith, D. (1997) Case Construction and the Goals of the Process. *The British Journal of Criminology*, 37(3): 319–46.

Smith, O. (2013) Court Responses to Rape and Sexual Assault: An Observation of Sexual Violence Trials, PhD thesis, University of Bath.

Smith, O. (2018) *Rape Trials in England and Wales*. London: Palgrave Macmillan.

Snedker, S. (2018a) Why the UK Needs a Separate Justice System for People with Mental Illness. [online] Theconversation.com. Available from: https://theconversation.com/why-the-uk-needs-a-separate-justice-system-for-people-with-mental-illness-98364 [Accessed 1 January 2020].

Snedker, S. (2018b) *Therapeutic Justice: Crime, Treatment Courts and Mental Illness*. Seattle, WA: Palgrave Macmillan.

Spigelman, J. (2001) The 'New Public Management' and the Courts. *Australian Law Journal,* 75: 1–46.

Sturge, G. (2023) *Court Statistics for England and Wales.* London: House of Commons Library.

Trade Union Council (2016) *Justice Denied: Impacts of the Government's Reforms to Legal Aid and Court Services on Access to Justice.* London: TUC.

Tyler, T. (2003) Procedural Justice, Legitimacy, and the Effective Rule of Law. *Crime and Justice,* 30: 283–357.

Tyler, T. (2007) Procedural Justice and the Courts. *Court Review,* 44: 26–31.

van Swaaningen, R. (1999) Reclaiming Critical Criminology: Social Justice and the European Tradition. *Theoretical Criminology,* 3(1): 5–28.

Vara, S. (2014) *North Liverpool Community Justice Centre Debate.* [online] Shaileshvara.com. Available from: https://www.shaileshvara.com/content/north-liverpool-community-justice-centre-debate [Accessed 8 January 2020].

Wacquant, L. (2012) *Punishing the Poor: The Neoliberal Government of Social Insecurity.* New York: Guilford Publication.

Walsh, K. (1995) *Public Service and Market Mechanisms.* London: Macmillan.

Ward, J. (2016) *Transforming Summary Justice: Modernisation in the Lower Criminal Courts.* London: Routledge.

Welsh, L. (2013) Are Magistrates' Courts Really a 'Law Free Zone'? Participant Observation and Specialist Use of Language. Papers from the British Criminology Conference, 3: 3–16.

Welsh, L. (2016) Magistrates, Managerialism and Marginalisation: Neoliberalism and Access to Justice in East Kent, PhD thesis, University of Kent.

Welsh, L. (2022) *Access to Justice in Magistrates' Courts: A Study of Defendant Marginalisation.* London: Bloomsbury Publishing.

Williams, A., Goodwin, M. and Cloke, P. (2014) Neoliberalism, Big Society, and Progressive Localism. *Environment and Planning,* 46: 2798–815.

Winick, B. and Wexler, D. (2003) *Therapeutic Jurisprudence and the Courts*. Durham, NC: Carolina Academic Press.

Woofitt, R. (2005) *Conversation Analysis and Discourse Analysis*. London: Sage Publishing.

Yin, R. (2003) *Case Study Research: Design and Methods* (4th edn). Los Angeles: Sage Publishing.

Index

References to endnotes show both the page number and the note number (231n3).

2007/8 financial crash 18

A

abuses of state power 4
accessibility 106
adversarialism
  feigned adversarialism 40–2
  solicitors' cooperativeness with each other 95
  solicitors prioritising 35
  true adversarialism 43–5
Albeit, Adisa 121n5
analytic interpretations 5, 16
Article 6(2) Human Rights Act 1998 100
artificial intelligence, use of 9
Auld, Lord 20–1, 31
Australia 97, 99

B

'bad character' evidence 17
'Big Society' (David Cameron) 19
bladed articles 70, 72, 102
Blair, Tony 17
Bradley Report (Department of Health) 29, 30, 111

C

Cameron, David 9, 19
capitalism 14
case management 94
  magistrates leaving court for 93–4
  solicitors' cooperative 32, 37–8
  streamlining of 20–1
  time-consuming nature of 40, 54
  see also cooperation between prosecution and defence
civil protection 4
competition between legal firms 19
Conservatives 12, 19
convicting the innocent 4, 24, 92
cooperation between prosecution and defence
  in the cause of speedy justice 21, 41–2
  promoting 112
  rather than adversarialism 95
  streamlining 20–1
  see also case management
costs in Criminal Cases (General Regulations 1986) 124n6
Court Estate Reform Programme 121n7
court staff
  defendants' means information 50
  defendants' mental health 56–9, 75–6, 99–100, 110, 122n9
  defendants seek clarity from 98, 109
  district judges insisting on speediness 34, 54
  effects on of Criminal Procedure Rules 21–2, 108
  more research needed on 112
  muting defendants using video conferencing 3–4, 26, 96, 115
  training required 110
  voicing dissatisfaction with procedures 74, 104
court workgroups 32–4, 45–8
  case management 38
  defendant management 32

defendants should be compensated for travel expenses 112
defendant's means information 50, 54, 98
dissatisfaction with procedures 73–4
district judges and 33, 96
mental health issues 56–60
self-representing defendants 53
speed of disposal causing problems 97–8, 109
too much routine 99–100
courthouse closures 2, 24–5, 112, 121n5
Courts Act 2003 21
cracked trials 23
crime control model 4
criminal justice
criticized for slowness 1
David Cameron 19–20
early guilty pleas 22–4
expenditure on 1
housing support 74, 111
interpreting efficiency 5, 118
L&D processes 29
mental health issues 100, 122n9
'new moral base' (Raine and Wilson) 15
process 6, 7–8
punishment within 7, 101
quality within 10–11
Raine and Willson 14–16
remanding 86
self-representing defendants 27
social justice and 120n4
streamlining 99
substance-related offenders 66, 94
Tony Blair and New Labour 17–18
two different models 3–4
undermining other sectors (through cost and inefficiency) 15
Criminal Justice Act 2003 17, 18
Criminal Procedure Rules (CPRs)
2005 21
2020 21
adversarial game-playing and 95
courts' drive for efficiency and 31
plea bargaining 108
prison sentences 111
quality justice threatened by 22
cross examination 43–5
of victims 80–3, 88–9, 105
traditional adversarialism in 54
Crown Courts
cases diverted from 17, 27
committals to 39–40, 47
re-victimisation 105, 117
Crown Prosecution Service 38, 95, 121n6

D

defence solicitors
apparently arguing for lengthier sentences 74–6, 78, 103–4, 111
CPS solicitors and 38, 40
rapid case disposals 95
see also solicitors
defendants
as victims 106
being caught a blessing 62–3
desiring to cure their addictions 76–7, 101
different views of on court procedure 98
disadvantaged defendants 72–4, 102, 104
fear of prison 23
management of 32
marginalised 21–2
means information 50
mental health issues 56–9, 75–6, 99–100, 110, 122n9
missing work and pay to attend court 83–5, 106
muted on video conferencing calls 3–4, 26, 96, 115
not allowed to speak 45–7, 96
providing them with a summary of court hearings 108–9
seeking clarity from court staff 97–8, 109
self-representation 27, 53
should be compensated for travel expenses 102

taking responsibility for their behaviour 64–6
victimisation of 106
delayed justice 9
Delivering Simple, Speedy, Summary Justice (Lord Falconer) 31
democracy 16
Department of Work and Pensions 115–16
depression 69, 71
disadvantaged people 67, 71–4, 102, 104, 113
disqualification from driving 52, 122–3n3
district judges 32–6, 45–8, 56–60
and amateur magistrates 28
apparent unfamiliarity with mental health procedures 59–60
defendants must take responsibility for their behaviour 64–6
disadvantaged defendants 102
encouraging guilty pleas 91
intimidatory interventions 33–4, 53–4
leadership practices 96
means information 50
plea-bargaining 91–3, 108
pressurising defence and prosecution 96
pro-active approach of 32–3
speedy justice games 96, 112
substance-related offenders 66
drug rehabilitation requirements (DRRs) 66–70, 102–3, 123n2 (Chapter 4), 123n3 (Chapter 5)
due process model 4, 22

E

early guilty pleas (EGPs) 22–4
drive for efficiency 31
giving a false guilty plea 87, 89, 105, 117
introduction of 2
quality justice and 92
efficiency
a defining issue 2
a question of priority 15
convictions of innocent people are inefficient 24
crime control model 4
delayed justice in the context of 9
different interpretations of 5
early guilty pleas 2
'economic efficiency and social justice' (Tony Blair) 17–18
efficiency and over-efficiency 3 *see also* over-efficiency
government reports emphasise importance 1
LASPO 26–7
lower courts a burden to court users 104
MacDonald on 5
managerial 19
multidimensional concept 8
New Labour's foundations for 16–17
Packer's concept of 4–5
putting concept into context 16
sale of courthouses 2
secondary role of 9, 10
speediness as 22
speediness over due process 17
two types of process 3–4
video conferencing 2–3
European Commission for the Efficiency of Justice (ECEJ) 97, 120–1 n5
evidence-in-chief 79–80, 88, 105
expenditure 1

F

fairness 15, 16
Falconer, Lord 31
false confessions 23–4, 87, 89, 105, 117
'fishing expeditions' 21
free market approach 13
funding 1

G

guilty pleas 36, 91 *see also* early guilty pleas

H

hearsay evidence 17
His Majesty's Courts and Tribunals Service (HMCTS) 1, 110, 115
Home Affairs Committee report 2004 107
homelessness 70, 71, 73–4, 111
human rights 91, 93, 120–1n5
Human Rights Act 1998 6, 8, 91, 100

I

ideal-types (Max Weber) 5, 120n3
individualism 121n1
innocent people convicted 3, 4, 24, 92 *see also* early guilty pleas
interpreters 7

K

key actions 20

L

laissez-faire 13
legal advisors 27, 36–7, 48–50, 54, 96, 114–15
legal aid
  applying for 26
  competition between solicitors 19–20
  LASPO 26, 31
  nature of 121n3
  proper working service needs 110
  solicitors' caseloads 95
Legal Aid and Advice Act 1949 121n3
Legal Aid, Sentencing and Punishment of Offenders Act 2012 (LASPO) 26–7, 116–17
Leveson, Lord 24–5, 30
liaison and diversion (L&D) services 29, 30, 111, 122n9
local organisations 19

M

MacDonald, S. 3, 4–6, 120ns1, 3, 4
magistrates
  absences from courtroom 41, 54, 93
  amateurs and professionals 20, 28, 68
  behavioural and moral governance on crime 14
  ill-equipped to navigate complex social issues 103
  laissez-faire approach 36–8
  means information 50
  mental health of defendants 58–9
  numbers 27
  reprimands from magistrates 101
Magistrates Courts
  austerity measures 19
  cases diverted to 27
  criticisms of 1
  Crown Court cases recategorized 17
  economic issues key 14
  expenditure 1
  fewer courts, fewer magistrates 27
  laissez-faire approach 36–7
  percentages of cases dealt with 1
  sending a case to the Crown Court 40
  single court researched by author 10
  streamlining procedures 20
managerialism
  at odds with courts' mission 14
  court workgroups 98
  managerial efficiency 19
  Raine and Willson 12
  streamlining 99
  see also speed-focused managerialism
means information 50–4, 98–9, 115
medication 56–7, 71
mental health issues 56–60, 70–2
  avoiding the issue 76, 99–100, 110
  courts overlooking signs of 110–11
  intertwined with substance abuse 30, 77
  L&D processes 29, 122n9

procedures to be taken 122n9
training required 111
Ministry of Justice 19, 31
mitigation
defence solicitors' approach 43
evidence for 109–10
prosecution solicitors avoid contesting 42, 54, 94–5
substance abuse and 60, 63, 76, 101
models of criminal justice processing 3–4
motivation 68–9, 87

N

National Audit Office 26
neoliberalism 12–13
New Labour 12, 16–19
New Public Management (NPM) 12
normative interpretations 5–6
North Liverpool Community Justice Centre (NLCJC) 30, 122ns10, 12

O

over-efficiency
cooperation, fact checking and 94
Criminal Procedure Rule and 22
district judges and amateur magistrates 28
examples of 9
magistrates stepping out of the courtroom 93
plea bargaining 92
proportionate sentencing 116
prosecution not contesting mitigation 109–10
rapid case disposals and 95–6
speed-focused managerial practices 54, 96
video links 97
overnight custody 86

P

Packer, H. 3–5, 15, 120n1
plea bargaining 24, 91–3, 108
pleas in mitigation *see mitigation*
police 4, 70, 120 ns1, 3
post-managerialism 12, 15–16
presumption of innocence 91, 100
prisons
apparently arguing for 74–6, 78, 103–4, 111
defendants' fear of 23
for the innocent 3
hostels for ex-prisoners 28
on remand 87, 107
private sector involvement 13
transporting to court 24–5
private sector 13
pro bono work 20
probation
attendance on 66, 67
in court 62, 72–4
private sector involvement 13
probation orders 70, 123n2 (Chapter 6)
reports 35–6, 61
problem-solving courts 29–30, 114, 122n9
procedural adversity 79, 85–8, 104–8
procedural due process 8–10, 16, 22, 93, 99, 118–19
prosecution solicitors
cracked trials 23
Criminal Procedure Rules 13
getting together with the defence 37, 42, 95, 96
mitigation of defence unchallenged 43, 54, 94
see also solicitors
public sector 13
public service cuts 18
punishment 101–3
financial 50
judicial process as 23, 98, 105
prison 78
rehabilitation and 103
remand as 107–8, 123n4
substance abuse, for 101

Q

quality justice
Criminal Procedure Rules's effect on 22

defendant comprehension 97
efficiency and 90, 92, 95, 118
magistrates' efforts 103
mental health issues 100
nature of 6–10
New Labour's failings 18
plea bargaining 93
post-hearing receipts 109
procedural adversity 104
Raine and Willson 16
remands, public safety and 117
self-representation and 116
substance addiction and 101

R

Raine and Willson 14–16, 18
rape victims 23
rapid disposal (of cases) 4, 9, 95, 99
rehabilitation
arguments for greater focus on 101
defence solicitors and 42, 111
magistrates are not experts 114
probation orders 123n2 (Chapter 4)
punishment and 103
substance abuse 48, 66, 70, 77, 102
remand 86–7
early guilty pleas and 105
pressure caused by 23, 89, 107–8, 117
responsibility for behaviour, taking 64–6, 70, 101
Review of Efficiency in Criminal Proceedings (Lord Leveson) 31
Review of the Criminal Courts of England and Wales (Lord Auld) 20, 31
'routinization' 21, 99

S

Sanders, A. 15–16
Schrödinger's cat 107, 123n4
self-control 66, 69
self-representation 26–7, 51–3, 116
sentencing
amateur magistrates 28
defendants missing paid work 85
disadvantaged defendants 72–4
for pleading guilty early 2, 22–3
homelessness 102
lifestyle choices and 65
long sentences 78, 103
means information 50, 98–9, 115
mental health issues 75–6, 100
mitigation against 43, 94–5, 109–10
plea bargaining 91, 93
process itself as 88
rehabilitation 121n8, 123n2 (Chapter 6)
remand set off against 86–7, 107
substance abuse and 60–1, 63, 65–6, 77, 101
Sentencing Council 2, 6, 22–3, 60
social housing 77, 113
social justice 7–10, 16–18
disadvantaged defendants 102, 104
low priority 22
magistrates' roles 28, 30, 113–14
meaning of 120n4
mental health and 100
rehabilitation and 101
social services 72, 114
social values 3, 5–7
socio-legal research 14
solicitors
adversarialism in use 35
case management 32
cross examination by 43–5, 80–1, 83
Crown Prosecution Service 95–6
district judge interrupting 33
examining victims 80, 82
legal aid solicitors 26, 31
on prison sentences 74–6, 78, 103–4, 111
on substance abuse 60–1
pressure on for a guilty plea 35–6
pro bono work 20
use of duress defence 34

working with the prosecution 21, 37–43, 54, 94, 95
specialist courts 29
specialisation 103
speed-focused managerialism 32, 35, 36–45, 53–4 *see also* managerialism
speediness 22
adversarialism and 45
defendant participation affected 96, 105, 109
district judges 53–4, 92
effect on defendants 22
fact checking and 94–5
New Labour prioritize 17
plea-bargaining 92–3
problem-solving courts 29
prosecution and mitigation 42
rapid case disposals 99
quality justice affected 97
video conferencing 2
standardized defendant processes 55, 78, 102
streamlining processes 20–1, 29
substance misuse 60–70
aggravating rather than mitigating factor 60–1, 63, 101
DRRs 123n2 (Chapter 4)
magistrates regard as morally reprehensible 63–5, 101
types of substance 123n1 (Chapter 4)
Suffolk 121n5
Swift and Sure Justice (Ministry of Justice White Paper) 31

T

three 'e's 13
timetables 20
Transform the CJS (Ministry of Justice) 19
'Transforming Summary Justice' courts (TSJ) 29–30
travelling to court 83–4, 106, 112

V

victim focused justice 22–4, 92–3
victims 79–83, 88–9
are they best served by defendants pleading guilty through plea bargaining 93
defendants as victims 106
improving the service to 121n6
justice process and 105–6
of rape 117
substance users 101
video conferencing 24–6
case study 49
continued expansion of 2
CPS views 121n6
effect on defendant participation 48, 50, 96–7, 115

W

Ward, J. 8
'warehouse disclosures' 21
Weber, Max 5, 120n3
White Papers 31
witnesses 23, 79, 89, 92, 117

Printed and bound by CPI Group (UK) Ltd, Croydon, CR0 4YY

20/08/2025

14722001-0001